D1081115

The
Book of
Angst

Gwendoline Smith is a clinical psychologist, speaker, blogger and the author of the books *The Book of Overthinking, The Book of Knowing, Depression Explained* and *Sharing the Load.* She also goes by the name Dr Know. Born and raised in Chatham, Kent, she now lives in Auckland, New Zealand.

The Book of Angst

Understand and Manage Anxiety

Gwendoline Smith

ALLEN&UNWIN

First published in Australia and New Zealand in 2021
by Allen & Unwin.

First published in Great Britain in 2022 by Allen & Unwin,
an imprint of Atlantic Books Ltd.

Copyright © Gwendoline Smith, 2021

The moral right of Gwendoline Smith to be identified as the author
of this work has been asserted by her in accordance with the
Copyright, Designs and Patents Act of 1988.

All rights reserved. No part of this publication may be reproduced,
stored in a retrieval system, or transmitted in any form or by any
means, electronic, mechanical, photocopying, recording, or otherwise,
without the prior permission of both the copyright owner and the
above publisher of this book.

10 9 8 7 6 5 4 3 2 1

A CIP catalogue record for this book is available from
the British Library.

Paperback ISBN: 978 1 83895 471 0
E-book ISBN: 978 1 83895 472 7

Text design by Megan van Staden
Illustrations by Georgia Arnold, Gabrielle Maffey and
Megan van Staden

Printed in Great Britain

Allen & Unwin
An imprint of Atlantic Books Ltd
Ormond House
26–27 Boswell Street
London
WC1N 3JZ

www.allenandunwin.com/uk

DEDICATION

Dr Lorna Breen, chair of the emergency medicine department at NewYork-Presbyterian Hospital, died as a result of self-inflicted injuries on 29 April 2020— the year that Covid-19 began to spread around the world. She had contracted Covid-19, but that was not how she died. She cared so much for her patients and her colleagues that the trauma of the epidemic eventually killed her.

After her death, her father asked that she be remembered and praised as a hero. Hence I dedicate *The Book of Angst* to Dr Breen, and to all health workers. I hope that you all make it through, and that we, your cousins in mental health, are able to do our best to help heal the psychic wounds of this global trauma.

CONTENTS

AUTHOR'S NOTE	8
INTRODUCTION: WHAT IS ANGST?	12

PART 1:
The Anxiety Family — 14

CHAPTER ONE
Generalised anxiety disorder (GAD) AKA
worrisome overthinking — 17

CHAPTER TWO
Obsessive-compulsive disorder (OCD) — 23

CHAPTER THREE
Post-traumatic stress disorder (PTSD) — 33

CHAPTER FOUR
Health anxiety (hypochondria) — 41

CHAPTER FIVE
Panic disorder — 51

CHAPTER SIX
The specific phobias — 63

CHAPTER SEVEN
The eating disorders — 75

CHAPTER EIGHT
Sexual response and anxiety — 85

CHAPTER NINE
The anxiety epidemic — 93

PART 2:
Social anxiety: the fear of judgement — 99

CHAPTER TEN
What is social anxiety? — 101

CHAPTER ELEVEN
More on social anxiety — 111

CHAPTER TWELVE
The biology of social anxiety — 127

CHAPTER THIRTEEN
Social anxiety and behaviour — 139

CHAPTER FOURTEEN
Performance, perfectionism,
procrastination and celebrity — 155

CHAPTER FIFTEEN
Emotion and thought — 167

PART 3:
Therapy time — 179

CHAPTER SIXTEEN
Therapy session one — 181

CHAPTER SEVENTEEN
Therapy session two — 203

CHAPTER EIGHTEEN
Therapy session three — 229

CHAPTER NINETEEN
Therapy session four — 249

CHAPTER TWENTY
Therapy session five — 259

CHAPTER TWENTY-ONE
Therapy session six — 269

CHAPTER TWENTY-TWO
Therapy session seven — 283

IMPORTANT STUFF TO REMEMBER — 295

APPENDIX: FLASHCARDS — 301

AUTHOR'S NOTE

I began writing *The Book of Angst* in April 2020 during the nationwide Covid-19 lockdown. When I had initially conceptualised this book, the virus was not yet a part of our lives. However, today we co-exist with a powerful pandemic, with the current leader of the free world suggesting the injection of disinfectant and exposure to UV light as potential remedies for this twenty-first-century plague.

Daily life has become surreal. Human beings, as a species hard-wired to attach and form close emotional bonds, are prohibited from such exchanges in our new and alien world. Millions of people worldwide have lost their jobs, their source of revenue, their ability to feed their families. Our health care workers are exposed to death trauma at a level never before seen during peacetime in living memory.

Our 'peacetime soldiers' have been risking their

lives every day to keep our basic needs taken care of: farmers, truck drivers, couriers, supermarket workers. As is so often the case, 'the little people' are on the front line, while billionaires sit in their mansions pining for their yachts and their Botox.

The current climate of our world is 'angst'. There is so much fear, so much concern, insecurity and uncertainty, created by life-threatening events of epidemic proportions. At the time this book went to print, there had been well over a million deaths worldwide.

The joyful news was that our magnificent natural kingdom had had a momentary reprieve from the toxicity of pollution caused by our human pursuits. Prior to Covid-19, 'eco-anxiety' was already a growing phenomenon in the first world—and it is not that our brothers and sisters in the developing world don't care, it's that they can't afford to care. How can refugees wash their hands twenty times a day when they have no water to drink?

Unfortunately the global environmental crisis has not gone anywhere—this is only a temporary remission. But during lockdown I have loved observing people out walking, admiring natural beauty, because they are forced to take the time to smell the flowers and the pollution-free air. I love seeing fathers out with their children bike-riding and being involved with them, probably in the highest numbers since the industrial revolution.

On social media I am comforted by the acts of 'coronavirus kindness', reinforcing that there is still great human altruism (perhaps not quite enough, but it's a start).

My other favourite posts are the ones of animals, birds and insects displaying their beauty, and watching them return to cleaner, more welcoming habitats.

I hope, with all my fingers and toes crossed, that we can make change and learn from this disaster. I would like to quote Sonya Renee Taylor, an author, poet, word artist, speaker, humanitarian, educator and social justice activator:

We will not go back to normal. Normal never was. Our pre-corona existence was not normal other than we normalized greed, inequity, exhaustion, depletion, extraction, disconnection, confusion, rage, hoarding, hate and lack. We should not long to return, my friends. We are being given the opportunity to stitch a new garment. One that fits all of humanity and nature.

—Sonya Renee Taylor

INTRODUCTION: WHAT IS ANGST?

The word 'angst' has existed since the eighth century. It is defined by the Merriam-Webster online dictionary as:

a strong feeling of being worried or nervous: a feeling of anxiety about your life or situation.

In this, *The Book of Angst*, I cannot possibly—and it has never been my intention to—address all of the varying forms of anxiety in detail. The focus of this book is on broadening your knowledge of the many manifestations of anxiety, with the intention of providing you with understanding, information and recommended treatment methods. You can dip in and out of the various chapters, paying particular attention to those pages where you think you might recognise a little bit of yourself or your loved one.

I have in the later chapters focused on **social anxiety disorder (AKA the fear of judgement)**. I have chosen this particular form of anxiety because it is so often misunderstood and under-diagnosed. Yet it is by far one of the most powerful and crippling of the many anxiety disorders.

In the section dedicated to social anxiety, I will discuss the many idiosyncratic features of this condition—those characteristics that make it stand apart from the others. I will provide understanding and education as well as treatment strategies.

The strategies in this book are based in cognitive behavioural therapy (CBT), which aims to help you manage your problems by changing how you think and act. These strategies can be utilised across the broad spectrum of anxiety conditions. If you identify with one or more of these conditions, it is vital that you seek professional help—particularly when it comes to the more debilitating of them, such as obsessive-compulsive disorder and post-traumatic stress disorder.

Read, have a laugh, and along the way you will hopefully learn some stuff that is both interesting and helpful. Now, come meet the 'Anxiety Family' . . .

PART 1

CHAPTER ONE

GENERALISED ANXIETY DISORDER (GAD)

AKA WORRISOME OVERTHINKING

This common disorder is characterised by persistent and excessive worry about a number of different things. People may anticipate disaster and be overly concerned about money, health, family, work or other issues. Thinking spirals incessantly, activated by the never-to-be-answered question 'what if?'

In these times of great uncertainty, worry is also at pandemic proportions—a manifestation of Covid-19. People are surrounded by things unknown, and all the elements of life that we once took for granted—safety, job security, financial security—are now uncertain. And uncertainty is fuel on the fire of worry.

I have observed that people diagnosed with generalised anxiety are more badly afflicted by their worrisome overthinking during the age of Covid-19, and others who have never previously been worriers have now become engaged with the practice.

WHAT IF?
OMG!
WHAT IF?
DISASTER!
OMG!
OMG!
WHAT IF?
IT WILL BE A DISASTER
IT WILL
WHAT IF?
OMG!

TREATMENT OPTIONS

Medication can be helpful with easing the distressing physical and emotional experiences of anxiety, although it does not offer a treatment per se.

If the long-term effects of the anxiety begin to manifest physically—for example, if your worrying is stopping you from sleeping, or you are experiencing gastrointestinal distress because of it (see page 80)—a pathway into depression can occur. This is where an antidepressant can be very helpful. If the depression has a significant anxiety component, an antidepressant with an anxiolytic (anti-anxiety) agent will most likely be prescribed.

Note: If you do seek medical advice at this stage, make sure that you explain your levels of anxiety to your doctor. Being prescribed the 'right' type of medication is essential. This is medication for your most important organ—the brain. It is not a matter of 'one size fits all'.

The recognised state-of-the-art intervention for worrisome overthinking is cognitive behavioural therapy (CBT). The treatment strategies work for both pre-existing and new converts (because of Covid-19) to the cyclical nature of worry.

If you relate to this condition and think you might need help, have a look at *The Book of Overthinking* (also written by me).

I would like to add that, in my opinion, worry is at the base of most of the various forms of anxiety. The anorexic worries about being fat, someone with OCD may worry about contamination, people with social anxiety worry about being judged.

I mention this because when treating the anxieties via CBT, therapists essentially take a two-pronged approach: addressing the worrisome overthinking alongside the specific content of the fear/phobia. This is very much the case with social anxiety.

OBSESSIVE-COMPULSIVE DISORDER (OCD)

Obsessive-compulsive disorder is an anxiety disorder in which sufferers have recurring, unwanted thoughts, ideas or sensations (**obsessions**) that make them feel driven to do something repetitively (**compulsions**). It is another profoundly debilitating anxiety condition. In fact once when I was at a neuroscience conference, one of the professors speaking stated that OCD was the most crippling of all of the anxiety conditions.

OCD is an especially difficult condition to treat, whether with medication, talk therapy or behavioural therapy. As a clinician, just when you think you have it nailed, back it comes—different thoughts, different behaviours, but the same torture.

In my opinion the reason that OCD is the giant of them all is because of its major genetic component. Overall, studies of twins with OCD estimate that genetics contributes 45-65 per cent of the risk of developing the disorder. A number of other factors may play a role in the onset of OCD, including behavioural, cognitive and environmental factors, but genetics is a biggie.

I have watched documentary material of three- and four-year-old children with OCD performing lengthy and complicated rituals that can take them hours to complete, and role-modelling doesn't appear to me to be a significant contributor.

> Whatever you do, don't blame
> yourself for your child's OCD.
> Even the worst parenting
> doesn't cause this disorder.

If you're a parent, OCD is not a 'phase' your child is going through. Nor is your son or daughter deliberately misbehaving or trying to get attention. Your child is not to blame.

Perhaps most importantly, it's not your fault if your child has OCD. OCD is a neurobiological disorder, which means that the brain of a child with OCD functions differently than the brain of a child who does not have OCD.

I have been practising for many, *many* years, and there have been phases in the psychological world of blaming parenting for children developing disorders such as OCD. During one such phase, which I recall occurring in the 1970s and beyond, there was very little acknowledgement of the complex relationship between nature and nurture, and that it was *not* either/or.

OCD manifests in many ways:
- checking
- fear of contamination
(fear of germs)
- hand-washing
- hoarding
- rumination
(thoughts going round in circles)
- intrusive thoughts.

When you look at this list you can begin to understand the profoundly destructive impact that OCD has on the daily lives of these poor souls and their families. Compulsive checking can go on for hours; extreme hoarding splits families and ruins lives. You can also begin to imagine the havoc that Covid-19 has created in the lives of people who struggle to live with OCD.

You can't ask an individual who compulsively washes their hands as a result of contamination phobia to stop doing it when the message to the entire globe is 'wash, wash and wash your hands again'. The difference is that the compulsive handwasher will scrub their hands until they bleed—standing fixated at the basin for hours, paralysed by fear.

The OCD brain demands the behaviour continues. Stopping results in unbearable anxiety for the afflicted. The only way to reduce the anxiety is to begin the ritual and repeat it again and again.

You see, it is the *subjective experience* of the anxiety that the individual wishes to escape. The worrisome, intrusive thoughts about contamination, or lack of symmetry, or throwing things away, create the anxiety, and then the compulsions are continued in an attempt to provide safety from the distress.

TREATMENT OPTIONS

Medication is almost always an option. However, I don't know of any medications that can 'cure' OCD. The options are **SSRIs** (selective serotonin reuptake inhibitors) or their new cousin **SNRIs** (serotonin-noradrenaline reuptake inhibitors), the difference being that the newer SNRIs work on both noradrenaline as well as serotonin in the brain.

In my experience, both do offer a certain amount of symptomatic relief. However, some of the older generation of medications (**tricyclics**) have also worked well, particularly if the condition is not too severe. I have also seen the **augmentation** of both generations of drugs provide assistance.

The easiest way to explain to you what **drug augmentation** means is to view it like making a cocktail. Pop some vodka, cranberry juice and ice into a glass and you've got a vodka and cranberry juice. Change the proportions, throw in some triple sec and lime juice, and you've got a Cosmopolitan.

So, you've got essentially the same ingredients, but pep it up with a touch of triple sec and you've got a bigger kick.

Pharmacological cocktails follow the same principles. Augmentation means that you can stick with the drug that is helping, but it gets given a booster shot. This prevents unnecessary and often unpleasant medication changes, and hopefully will enhance the workings of the original compound.

Because of the insidious nature of OCD, these types of medication adjustments are not unusual.

When someone living with OCD presents to me in my psychology practice, I will more often than not, depending on the severity of their condition, refer them to a psychiatrist to start on medication as the first port of call. Hopefully once the medication has provided some symptom relief, I can begin work within the CBT modality.

The emphasis with this group of people is on the **behavioural** component of CBT. Cognitive strategies can be helpful, but exposure to the feared situations usually makes the most impact.

A book that I have had in my library for many years is *Brain Lock: Free Yourself from Obsessive-Compulsive Behavior*, by Jeffrey M. Schwartz. I highly recommend this book to OCD sufferers, as do many of my clients who have read it.

To be honest with you, we have not yet discovered the optimal treatment for OCD. However, a combination of the above does without doubt contribute to an improvement.

POST-
TRAUMATIC
STRESS
DISORDER
(PTSD)

According to Wikipedia, PTSD is:

a mental disorder that can develop after a person is exposed to a traumatic event, such as sexual assault, warfare, traffic collisions, child abuse, or other threats on a person's life. Symptoms may include disturbing thoughts, feelings, or dreams related to the events, mental or physical distress to trauma-related cues, attempts to avoid trauma-related cues, alterations in how a person thinks and feels, and an increase in the fight-or-flight response.

We first learned about this condition through the after-effects of warfare. After World War I it was known as 'shell-shock'. Research on the condition began to gain significant pace after the Vietnam War, when veterans returned home drug-addicted and disillusioned.

The whole city of New York was traumatised by

the attack on the Twin Towers on 11 September 2001. Mental-health workers were at Ground Zero, counselling survivors with PTSD, and schools introduced resiliency training as part of their compulsory curriculum.

There is no way of estimating the post-traumatic impact of Covid-19 on our health workers, our frontline peacetime soldiers, who overseas have had to find resting places for tens of thousands of lifeless bodies—but it will be phenomenal.

It is interesting to note that in times of crisis human beings seem to find the wherewithal and the determination to keep going. This is certainly the case with Covid-19. Day after day, health workers return to the horror of the front line, still trying to save lives, risking their own and their families'.

PTSD, as its name implies, occurs *post* (after) the trauma. It is more often the case that, as the crisis subsides, PTSD is a petri dish for the germination of exhaustion, obsessive rumination and **flashbacks**: frightening memories of death or near-death echoing through the ears (auditory), the nose (olfactory), the eyes (visual) and the soul.

Flashbacks can be experienced
through multiple senses.

I would like to take time here to highlight the devastating experience of the flashback. When these occur, the brain thinks it is back in the terrifying, life-threatening situation. The nervous system goes back in time, and the trauma is not just remembered but *relived*. The intensity of the overwhelming nature of the flashback must never be underestimated. This is why the avoidant behaviour found in PTSD is so profound—it is the method sufferers use to stay away from re-experiencing the horror.

Early in my career I did a stint in America in a drug-rehabilitation facility. I remember vividly the wailing from the group therapy room when the Vietnam vets would get together. It was a closed meeting, as the pain, as well as their shame, was too much to share with civilians, including therapists.

But the case of PTSD that I learned the most from, and will remember for the rest of my life, like it was yesterday, is this one. It involved a wonderful, courageous man, who was a first-responder in Phuket following the Boxing Day tsunami in 2004, which left an estimated 230,000 people dead.

As we got to know each other during therapy, he would tell me what it was like walking through dunes of dead bodies. There were little children with their water-wings still on. It was holiday time, and the weather was sunny and tropically hot. What he recalled the most, and what haunted him every waking hour—and flashbacked when he put his head down at night—was the stench of rotting bodies.

As I mentioned above, all of our senses have memories. A picture may be worth a thousand words, but as far as I am concerned no painting or photograph could ever capture stench.

I was part of a team of mental-health professionals working with people like this man, and we made a difference. I can't tell you where he is now, but I do know that he has a new life that he loves. (Whew, that part was hard to type!)

TREATMENT OPTIONS

Because of the prevalence of nightmares and flashbacks, sleeping medication is often prescribed, along with mild tranquilisers for daytime anxiety. Antidepressants can be helpful, often alongside some of the more gentle antipsychotics, to help with intrusive thoughts. (I call these 'thought managers'—a far more elegant term than anti-psychotics, in my opinion.)

Psychological therapy is essential. There are three main types of psychological therapies used to treat people with PTSD:

- cognitive behavioural therapy (CBT),
- eye-movement desensitisation and reprocessing (EMDR), and
- group therapy.

I am not recommending any particular one of these therapies. I believe that what works and is safe for each person is the 'right' therapy.

I work as part of a multi-disciplinary team, and am a believer in that approach. Each discipline has something to contribute to these highly complex conditions. Treatment is no longer an either/or situation—both psychological therapies and pharmacology play a part.

However, I cannot emphasise enough how essential professional help is to treat this anxiety condition. There have always been, and continue to be, suicides in response to PTSD (as referred to in the dedication to this book).

HEALTH ANXIETY (HYPO- CHONDRIA)

This is obsessive and irrational worry about having a serious medical condition. It's also called illness anxiety, and was formerly called hypochondria. This condition is marked by a person's imagining physical symptoms of illness or, in other cases, their misinterpretation of minor or normal body sensations as serious disease symptoms, despite reassurance by medical professionals that they don't have an illness. Reassurance-seeking behaviour does nothing to help this condition, but does provide temporary relief after the medical appointment.

If your body is sending you signs that you're ill, it's normal to be concerned. However, health anxiety is marked by constant belief that you have a symptom or symptoms of a severe illness. You may become so consumed by worry that the distress becomes disabling and interferes with your quality of life.

Individuals with health anxiety spend not only a lot of time with their doctors but also an excessive amount of time consulting Dr Google—much to the dismay of general practitioners.

Let's talk about freckles and moles for a moment—a classic arena for misinterpretations and faulty self-diagnoses. I would like you to meet Milly (a hypothetical patient), who suffers with health anxiety and is looking at some marks on her skin.

Facts:

1. Freckles are small, usually pale brown areas of skin.

2. Moles are areas of darker pigmented skin (brown or brown/black).

Health anxiety perspective:

Milly: So they're both brown. How am I supposed to know what defines pale brown and what brown/black looks like? This one I'm looking at on my arm looks like a cross between pale brown and brown/black. Better Google . . . this looks interesting . . .

Almost everyone has skin moles, and most of them are harmless. But as they come in so many shapes, sizes and colours, it can be hard to know whether moles are normal. While most moles are nothing to be concerned about they can, rarely, become cancerous.

—www.molesonline.com

Milly: 'Rarely become cancerous'? That means I could be the rare one!

Milly's heart is racing and her temperature is rising. Her breathing is becoming shallow.

Milly: Right, time to refine the Google search . . .

OMG: 142 million hits!!!!

> **Milly**: WTF am I supposed to do with that?! I think I'll go back to those UnityPoint people—they seemed to know what they were doing. I can't leave it too much longer otherwise I'll miss out on getting an appointment.

Milly is now getting increasingly anxious. She can't remember what size or colour her mole was yesterday. This is more than she can cope with.

Her doctor reassures her that it looks fine. That reassurance may last Milly a few days or even a week, but the problem with reassurance-seeking in cases of health anxiety is that it doesn't last.

Her attention will return to the diagnosed-as-harmless pale brownish, blackish, possibly asymmetrical blemish on her arm, and off she goes to have it looked at by a dermatologist.

Once again, the battle is with the **subjective discomfort** of the anxiety (Milly's experience of how it makes her feel—more on this later). Worrying about the blemish creates anxiety, then Milly begins to predict the worst possible outcomes—having her arm removed because of a cancerous melanoma, in her mind removing all chances of getting married or being able to hold and breastfeed a baby in the future.

Point of interest: Attentional focus

I would like to introduce you now to this very important phenomenon (applicable to all forms of anxiety). A major part of the reason that Milly is in this state of anxiety is the constant **attention** she is giving the blemishes on her skin.

So do this experiment with me—it is something that people with anxiety are doing all the time, without even realising it. Here we go, follow these instructions:

OK, swallow now.

Swallow one more time.

And swallow again.

Your mouth gets more and more dry, and it becomes so awkward it's as though you've never swallowed before—almost like you are trying to swallow a camel.

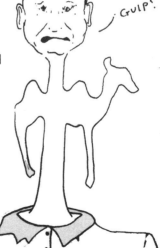

47

This **subjective experience**—that lump in your throat that you personally feel—has occurred because of your intense focus on what is usually an involuntary response.

The eyes do a similar thing, called 'auto-reticular recognition'. It goes something like this:

You've decided to treat yourself to a new car. You've decided on your price range, you've picked the brand, you've gone for electric. All that has to be decided on is the colour, which often tends to be where women start (it's true!). After much deliberation you go for a white car—not too hot in summer, and a colour you don't see too often. You drive off the car lot and much to your horror . . . every second car appears to be white.

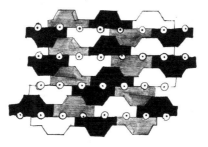

So, as you can begin to see, the brain and our senses are playing tricks on us all the time, though we are not aware of it.

If we go back to Milly for a moment, on her way to the mole-mapping clinic every second billboard seems to be about skin cancer, and every third billboard about raising funds for the Cancer Society. Here again, this is Milly's perception—just like the white cars and the struggle with swallowing.

TREATMENT OPTIONS

Once more, psychological therapies such as CBT offer the most assistance when dealing with health anxiety. Medications can provide some assistance in settling the physically distressing symptoms that occur as a function of any of the anxiety conditions, including health anxiety.

I have successfully treated many individuals with health anxiety. The approach is very similar to the treatment for worrisome overthinking. The main adjustment is to incorporate the worry about health as the specific focus.

CHAPTER FIVE

PANIC DISORDER

ost people will experience a panic attack at least once or twice in their lives, according to the American Psychological Association. But panic disorder is characterised by the persistent fear of having another attack. It is officially defined as experiencing at least one month (or more) of persistent concern or worry about additional panic attacks (or their consequences).

You may be having a panic (anxiety) attack when you feel sudden, overwhelming terror that has no obvious cause. You may experience physical symptoms, such as a racing heart, breathing difficulties and sweating. This may be a result of exhaustion, overdoing things, not getting enough sleep, a new baby in the family—all sorts of ambiguous reasons.

First, you get a fright because your startle/survival response mechanism is switched on unexpectedly. Then you attend to the sensations (good old attentional focus at work), misinterpret the potential explanations for the sensations and begin to magnify the seriousness of what is occurring.

Then, as you begin to panic, the experience becomes driven by fear, most often the fear of death or of going insane. A trip to the doctor may, and often does, result in medical assessments, as the racing heart could be taken as a symptom of a heart attack. Off you go to the cardiologist.

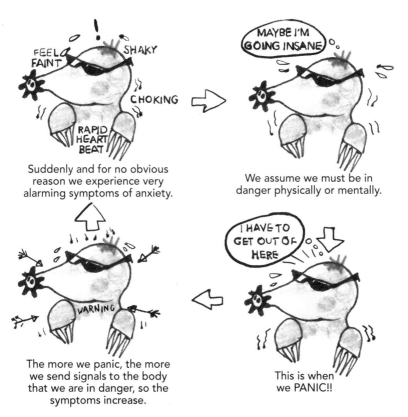

Suddenly and for no obvious reason we experience very alarming symptoms of anxiety.

We assume we must be in danger physically or mentally.

The more we panic, the more we send signals to the body that we are in danger, so the symptoms increase.

This is when we PANIC!!

Heaps of explorations later the results come back negative: heart good, blood pressure good, respiratory function good. Then the to-be-expected question from the health practitioner: 'Do you have a history of anxiety?'

Initially this can be a very difficult question to deal with. It is often as though the clinician is minimising your discomfort and saying that it is all in your mind.

I remember when I worked in a chronic pain clinic back in the 1980s. It was called the Psychosomatic Pain Clinic. Patients hated that name, because they believed that this implied that the pain was all in their head and wasn't real.

What is important to note is that *the physical sensations that are experienced are real.* However, they are not caused by physical problems.

Once a clean bill of physical health is declared, the challenge lies in learning to deal with what is happening in your psychological world. The trap now is the cycle of fear that can develop as a result of the attack.

As I mentioned earlier, one isolated incident can develop into a panic disorder because of the persistent fear and ongoing worry that the event may recur. I have seen this morph into situations where lives are debilitated and dominated by fear and avoidance.

I treated one of my most memorable cases of panic disorder when I was working in America in the early 1980s: a mother of two who presented with cocaine addiction and OCD (let's call her Gillian). Her husband was unable to cope with her behaviour and brought her to the treatment programme where I was training.

Once her drug detox was complete and she had settled into the therapeutic community, she asked me if I would accompany to her home, as she had some decluttering of her life to take care of. Her teenage daughters and her husband were there, waiting eagerly for our arrival.

The house did look very cluttered, but so do a lot of family homes. Then I was escorted downstairs to a basement the size of a small warehouse. I stood in a state of disbelief, staring at rack after rack after rack, box after box of clothing, bedding, crockery, cutlery . . . it was like a secret department store.

I noticed on my way out after that first visit that the house was not just cluttered—it was packed full of purchases that had never even been unwrapped. It took several visits to 'declutter' everything, as each item had to be considered carefully prior to being given away to charity.

When we got back to the treatment facility, I had a debriefing session with Gillian, in which I asked her how her life had evolved in that way. In summary, her reply went like this:

After the birth of our second daughter, I was hanging out the washing when I had a panic attack. The girls were close together in age, so I do remember being sleep-deprived a lot of the time.

After the first attack, I began to live in fear of another attack, so I would get my husband to do all of the shopping. I then became unable to go to the supermarket, and this was followed by my becoming agoraphobic. I then developed a fear of being in contact with other people.

My husband liked to gamble, and we would go to Las Vegas a few times a year. We both liked cocaine, and I found that the only way I could deal with going out was to be high. I wasn't a gambler, so the girls and I would go shopping instead.

The purchasing became increasingly compulsive. I could never make decisions, so if I liked a dress, I would buy it in every colour they had and every size, as my weight would fluctuate like a yo-yo. That's when the hoarding started.

I would get all the merchandise home and have to make space for everything. If my husband challenged what I was doing it would end up in a huge argument.

I could see the pain my girls were going through—they could never bring friends home to see what their crazy mother was doing. So finally I decided to get help.

Get the picture? From one panic attack to all of that! That's how powerful the condition can be—how powerful the mind can be.

Note: If anyone ever minimises what you are experiencing as a result of your anxiety, tell them in the nicest possible way to

Gillian is an example of someone having what we in the trade call **comorbidity**. This is when more than one of the Anxiety Family members move into your headroom. (Comorbidity is such a horrible word, I know. A nicer term, I think, is coexisting.)

If we go back to Gillian, she started with an anxiety attack, which morphed into panic disorder, which then developed into agoraphobia, compulsive hoarding and then cocaine addiction.

Wow, five different conditions all coexisting. Hence, the treatment approach needed to be multi-disciplinary. Her addiction was addressed in the treatment facility, in combination with the AA 12-step programme. This helped not only with her addiction but also with her compulsive purchasing habits. She participated in both group and individual psychotherapy, along with **in vivo desensitisation**. This is a technique used in behaviour therapy, usually to reduce or eliminate phobias, in which the client is exposed to stimuli that induce anxiety. For Gillian, this involved going through all the objects and clothes that she had hoarded to enable her to tolerate the anxiety created by the thought of getting rid of something.

TREATMENT OPTIONS

In those days, cognitive behavioural therapy was not widely practised, so the above were the available treatment options. These days, however, Gillian would have had pharmacology (medication) and CBT in her treatment package. I don't know how she is now, but I hope she's OK.

Even though the symptoms of panic disorder can be quite overwhelming and frightening, they can be managed and improved with treatment. Asking for professional help is the most important thing you can do to reduce your symptoms and improve your quality of life.

As with the other anxiety conditions, medication can provide some symptom relief. If the worry and anxiety can be reduced, it leaves you better equipped to engage with the talk therapy.

Again, CBT remains the leading-edge treatment methodology for anxiety, including panic disorder. With panic disorder, **behavioural exposure** is an important element of the cognitive behavioural approach. That is why it was so important to visit Gillian's home and go through her hoard of clothing and other items.

CHAPTER
SIX

THE SPECIFIC PHOBIAS

Now this is where the palette expands ad infinitum! The foundations of this group are the same as the previously discussed phobias.

Specific phobias are an overwhelming and unreasonable fear of objects or situations that pose little real danger but provoke anxiety and avoidance. Unlike the brief anxiety you may feel when giving a speech or taking a test, specific phobias are long lasting, cause intense physical and psychological reactions, and can affect your ability to function normally at work, at school or in social settings.

—Mayo Clinic

There are many, many types of phobias, which can also coexist with other forms of anxiety, for example:

- airplanes—flying, enclosed spaces
- going to school

- thunderstorms
- heights
- animals—spiders, insects, dogs, rats
- medical procedures—blood, injections, needles, accidents
- choking, vomiting
- loud noises
- clowns.

Or, to use technical terms:

- aerophobia (flying)
- astraphobia (thunder and lightning)
- acrophobia (heights)
- arachnophobia (spiders)
- haemophobia (blood)
- autophobia (being alone)
- hydrophobia (water)
- agoraphobia (fear of spaces where there is no escape).

What the phobia is focused on will determine its degree of interference with daily life. For example, a fear of flying prohibits long-distance travel; a fear of heights can be avoided by not going hiking up steep mountains and not looking out of the windows when in a tall building. With a fear of elevators, which can trigger claustrophobia and agoraphobia, a sufferer might use the stairs even if they have to climb twenty flights. Anything to avoid the anxiety!

TREATMENT OPTIONS

It is very rare that medication will be prescribed for simple phobias, unless they are coexisting with another, more debilitating anxiety disorder. Minor tranquilisers are often prescribed for fear of flying, to enable people to get through the flight and have a snooze.

Cognitive behavioural therapy—with a *big* emphasis on behaviour—is the primary treatment. You see, before the C (cognitive) existed in CBT we were trained as behaviourists (B)—the cognitive approach came much later. We would use exposure to the feared objects or situations as treatment. For example: if you have a fear of flying, the goal of the therapy is to get you on the plane.

We would achieve these therapeutic goals by a

process called 'systematic desensitisation'—in other words, systematically introducing the patient to the feared situation (using baby steps). This was very effective, and the behavioural approach still contributes a great deal to the treatment of many of the phobias, whether they be simple or complex.

A REALLY FUNNY STORY . . .

I thought this would be a good time in *The Book of Angst* to introduce a bit of light relief, so here we go. This is a personal anecdote from my days of being an intern—a real baby therapist with no experience, clumsy and going by the seat of my pants.

As part of my academic qualifications I had to complete a case history of a successful treatment intervention. Phobias were always a safe bet, as they were specific and responded well to the behavioural treatment modalities of the time.

I got on the phone to a number of old mates and was given the name of a guy called Charles who had a spider phobia. *Perfect!* I thought to myself, completely forgetting the essential fact that I also had a spider phobia, untreated. Continuing to be unfazed by the truth, I made contact with Charles.

'Hi Charles, it's Gwendoline Smith here. A colleague of mine who is a friend of yours told me that you wouldn't mind getting a hand with your spider phobia?'

'Yes, he mentioned that you would be calling.'

'Great—why don't I come over on Monday evening?'

'That will be fine.' And he gave me his address.

The chosen therapeutic technique was systematic desensitisation, as outlined above. The idea was to gently expose the individual to the feared object, keeping their anxiety down through relaxation and breathing techniques. The degree of anxiety is measured by a pulse meter attached to the thumb, providing measurements of any increase in heart rate (a biofeedback mechanism).

Monday evening arrived and I headed off to meet Charles with a few books of spider pictures and the pulse meter. I hooked Charles up and put one of the spider pictures in front of him. Vigilantly looking at the biofeedback machine, I couldn't help but notice that there was no movement. But I desperately needed to collect a clinical baseline.

Charles interrupted me and said, 'Gwendoline, spider pictures don't really bother me.'

I replied, 'Charles, it's important that we don't rush this.'

Important for me, especially, with the case study being the main focus.

He went on to say, 'Only real spiders bother me.'

Me again: 'Charles, it's really important that we take it easy at this stage of the treatment.'

I left, troubled as to how this case study was going to go, but determined not to give up. This was my final exam, my ticket to a clinical diploma.

The following Monday, I turned up at Charles's house, this time with a real live spider in a jar with the lid on. I hooked Charles up to the biofeedback apparatus and moved the jar with the spider in it closer and closer to his face. Still nothing—no recording, no increase in pulse. *F@ck!* I thought to myself.

Charles muttered, 'Gwendoline, I don't mind if the spider is in a jar with a lid on—it's more if I can see it running free.'

Now f@cking what? I thought. I then asked Charles if he had a container that I could put the spider in. We rummaged around in the kitchen and came up with a two-litre ice cream container. Plenty of room for the free-range spider.

Off we went back into the lounge. I hooked him up to the pulse meter and held the container with the spider in it, moving it slowly closer to his face (remembering this is a desensitisation technique).

Busily looking at the pulse meter to record the data for the case study, I forgot I was still holding the ice cream container.

'Gwendoline . . .' said Charles.

'What!?' I replied impatiently.

'The spider is climbing out of the tub towards your finger.'

I screamed, dropped the tub and leapt onto a chair. 'Kill the f@cking thing!' I exclaimed. Charles whacked the spider with a magazine and the session came to a close.

Highly embarrassed, I got down off the chair and said to Charles, 'Sorry about that. I'll see you next week.'

This was a nightmare!

I told my boyfriend of the time about my dilemma. He offered to fix the problem. Through exposure, I got to the point where I could have

the spider running up and down my arm with no anxiety; I could have worn it as an earring. Perfect!

So with my own phobia treated using the exposure technique, I was really looking forward to my next session with Charles. I arrived with a spider in a jar—not that it needed to be by that stage, with my new-found confidence.

'OK, Charles—buckle up, let's go.' On went

the pulse meter and out came the spider, placed delicately in the palm of my hand.

As I moved my hand closer and closer to Charles, still vigilantly observing the pulse meter, he piped up and said, 'Gwendoline, could I hold the spider?'

No, of course you f@cking can't, I have nowhere near the data I need! I thought to myself. But what I said was: 'Are you sure, Charles? It's important that we don't rush this.'

'No, I'm sure,' he replied. 'If you can touch the spider after last week, anybody can.'

Oh well—it was a successful intervention, but not quite following the path I'd had in mind!

CHAPTER
SEVEN

THE EATING
DISORDERS

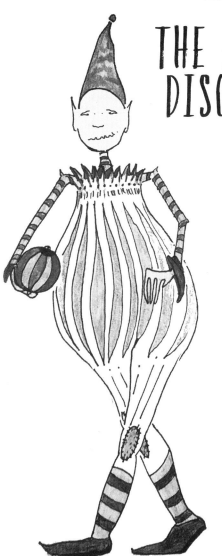

ow I have introduced you to the most talked-about members of the Anxiety Family. However, it is my clinical opinion that anxiety sits at the base of the many psychological afflictions of humanity.

Take, for example, the eating disorders or, as a client described it for me once, 'disorderly eating'. The anorexic is desperately trying to control their feelings of anxiety and powerlessness in the world by starving themselves. The bulimic is trying to comfort themselves through binge eating, but then purging, constantly tortured by the guilt.

Studies suggest that eating disorders and anxiety disorders coexist more often than not. Around two-thirds of people with an eating disorder also suffer from an anxiety disorder. The anxiety condition most commonly associated with eating disorders in general is obsessive-compulsive disorder (OCD), but the link between anxiety and eating disorders is seen in people with a range of both types of conditions. In an article on health.com, Amanda Gardner writes:

> *In most cases, people say the anxiety came first. And although no one can say with 100% certainty why the link exists, most thinking points to a need for a sense of control. You could almost think of the eating disorder as a symptom of the anxiety.*

TWO OUT OF THREE PEOPLE WITH AN EATING DISORDER SUFFER FROM SOME TYPE OF ANXIETY.

This is certainly my clinical experience. My clients recall an anxious childhood and then, usually in puberty, for many different reasons, the desire to control the anxiety morphs into a destructive relationship with food.

You may be thinking (or then again, you may not):

How come this doesn't happen to all kids and teenagers? They are exposed to the same media, full of images of the perfect body, with the perfect skin, with hundreds of thousands of followers on Instagram.

This is where genetics plays a part. Genetics and family history may create a predisposition to a phenomenon we refer to as **high trait anxiety**. This is where the subjective experience of any form of distress (anxiety) is more intense and takes longer to resolve. Theorists estimate a genetic influence of between 25 and 40 per cent, depending on the

type of anxiety and the age group being studied.

More research is being conducted on the possible genetic contribution to anorexia in particular. Although nothing definitive has been revealed so far, it would appear that it is more than a psychosocially based condition (one related to the person's environment).

'BRAIN IN THE GUT'

Neurogastroentorology is a branch of research which takes the view that there is something biological going on with people with eating disorders. In my opinion, the link comes via an anxiety pathway. Let me explain . . .

We place so much emphasis on how we feel internally that people talk about their 'gut feelings' and make decisions based on them. Yes, we do experience 'gut feelings', but given that 95 per cent of our serotonin receptors reside in the gut it's hardly surprising.

This is where neuroscience gets really fascinating. I bet you didn't know that we have brain cells in the digestive tract (AKA the enteric nervous system).

These neurons are referred to as the 'second brain', additional to the brain at the top of the spinal cord. New research now suggests that these neurons may actually be the very first 'brain' that our mammalian ancestors evolved.

Dr Emeran Mayer wrote in *The Mind-Gut Connection* that this connection between the two brains lies at the heart of many afflictions, both physical and psychiatric, such as anxiety, depression, ulcers and irritable bowel syndrome.

Research also shows that the majority of individuals with anxiety and depression will also have disturbance in their gastrointestinal system.

So when I say anxiety impacts adversely on your health, and in particular the gastrointestinal system—causing conditions such as those listed above—I'm not joking. (If you're interested in the research on the 'second brain' it's well worth reading the article 'A brain in the head, and one in the gut' by Harriet Brown in the *New York Times*, August 2005—Google it.)

Just to explain this a little further from another angle: when the 'fight/flight/freeze' survival mechanism is switched on, by either a real or a perceived threat, Mother Nature essentially shuts down the digestive system so that the body can divert all its internal energy towards facing the threat and ensuring our survival. Hence, the goal is not to stop and eat—it is to survive, not indulge.

The point being that your body's priority is survival, even when the threat is perceived and not real, such as when someone with an eating disorder gets on the scales and finds they have put on weight. Having your gut knot up for a few minutes might be almost desirable for those of us feeling a bit chubby, but it is daunting and disastrous for the anorexic in recovery.

I am reminded of a wonderful BBC documentary I watched many years ago, which portrayed a group of young females in a live-in eating-disorder rehabilitation centre. The girls' weight on admission varied among the group, but the young woman I remember was admitted at a weight of 45 kg (99 lb). Her recommended weight, taking into account her height and BMI (body mass index), was set at 65 kg (143 lb). With a great deal of blood, sweat and tears, determination and wonderful treatment staff, she reached her goal weight and was discharged. This was an incredible achievement, given her degree of anorexic body distortion and the fear of being 'fat'.

But when she returned to her studies at Oxford University and was hit with the first wave of perfectionistic-based performance anxiety, almost immediately her gut knotted up and she had no appetite. Her weight once again started to plummet.

I remember what she said to camera:

'I feel as though I have been betrayed by my body. It's as though my body is stopping me from eating.'

And that was what was happening. With the rise in her anxiety levels, her digestive system began to close down.

There is a strong link between anxiety and eating disorders. If someone is feeling powerless and anxious about the pressures of the world around them, controlling their food intake is a way of reclaiming some power.

TREATMENT OPTIONS

I'm not sure how much emphasis was placed on dealing with anxiety in the rehab programme above, but these days we look at utilising anxiolytic antidepressants (antidepressants that also work on treating anxiety), along with CBT for anxiety and stress management and group therapy.

CHAPTER
EIGHT

SEXUAL RESPONSE AND ANXIETY

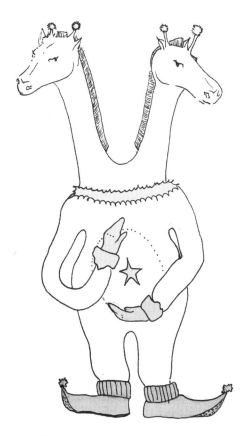

This is an area often overlooked when discussing anxiety. I haven't practised much in the way of sex therapy, but what I do know as a specialist in anxiety is that there is an inextricable link between it and sexual response. Let me introduce you to some of the basic theory in this area.

Note: I would like to emphasise that in this discussion I am talking about human sexuality in general, regardless of what form of sexual intimacy between humans that may involve.

CATEGORIES

Sexual dysfunction generally is classified into four categories:

- desire disorders—lack of sexual desire or interest in sex
- arousal disorders—inability to become physically aroused or excited during sexual activity
- orgasm disorders—delay or absence of orgasm (climax)
- pain disorders—pain during intercourse.

SYMPTOMS

Male:

- inability to achieve or maintain an erection suitable for intercourse (erectile dysfunction)
- absent or delayed ejaculation despite adequate sexual stimulation (retarded ejaculation)
- inability to control the timing of ejaculation (early or premature ejaculation).

Female:

- inability to achieve orgasm
- inadequate vaginal lubrication before and during intercourse
- inability to relax the vaginal muscles enough to allow intercourse.

All genders:

- lack of interest in or desire for sex
- inability to become aroused
- pain with intercourse.

The golden rule with most psychological health conditions is to initially rule out any physiological causes of the condition. Many physical and/ or medical conditions can cause problems with sexual function, including diabetes, heart and vascular (blood vessel) conditions, neurological disorders, hormonal imbalances, and chronic diseases such as kidney or liver failure.

Alcoholism and drug abuse can also affect sexual function, as can the side-effects of some medications, including some antidepressant drugs. This side-effect often means people, particularly men, do not remain compliant with antidepressant medication (they stop taking it). As far as I am aware drug manufacturers have not managed to overcome this challenge; some companies claim they have, but their antidepressants don't do what they're supposed to either. Go figure!

Psychological causes of sexual dysfunction include concern about sexual performance, work- or relationship-related stress and anxiety, body-image issues, past sexual abuse or trauma, and depression. So, as you can see, the psychological contribution to sexual disfunction is not insignificant, nor is the role of anxiety. Performance anxiety is a major issue in the psychological domain: if things don't go too well on one occasion (for one of many possible reasons), a self-fulfilling cycle can occur, where fear of ongoing issues can actually start to cause them.

Sexual performance anxiety

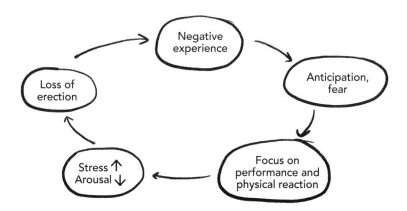

One other phenomenon that I will introduce you to, which is very anxiety-based, is 'spectatoring', a process first identified by Masters and Johnson (see overleaf) in 1970. This is where one or both of the partners start to engage in sex from a third-person perspective—as if looking from above at their participation in the act. These thoughts distract from the sexual activity, which requires a focus on sensation.

TREATMENT OPTIONS

When I was training to be a psychologist in the 1970s, we were required to study *Human Sexual Response* and *Human Sexual Inadequacy*, two pioneering books from the team of Drs William Masters and Virginia Johnson (subjects of a great Netflix series, if you get a chance to watch it). In those days there were very few specialist practitioners in the field of psychology in this country, so we tended to be more like general practitioners.

Now, many years later, there are many specialised sex therapists (sexologists). The research into human sexuality conducted by Masters and Johnson all those decades ago still remains an important foundation of sex therapy. These techniques are primarily behavioural, with an emphasis on relaxation and encouraging sensuality, taking away the pressure to perform. This technique is referred to as 'sensate focus'.

Anecdotally, I have had male clients who find the use of drugs such as Viagra helpful. This form of intervention can be helpful in reducing premature ejaculation and in breaking the psychologically based anxiety cycle.

CHAPTER NINE

THE ANXIETY EPIDEMIC

A few observations before we move on . . .

For many years my primary clinical focus was depression. I wrote two books on the topic, *Sharing the Load* (1996) and a rewrite in 2002, *Depression Explained*. At the time, depression and suicide were being spoken of as occurring in epidemic proportions while, as I recall it, anxiety was rarely spoken about in this way. Now, however, World Economic Forum statistics show the number-one mental-health concern that people face is anxiety, with an estimated 275 million sufferers—so if it affects you, you are far from being alone.

As the years have passed, and the number of clients I am working with has increased, it has become clear to me that anxiety is the true epidemic. Depression occurs more often than not when the system starts to shut down as the end result of long-term untreated anxiety. You see, the anxiety response is a survival response—it is not supposed to be activated in the system over the long term.

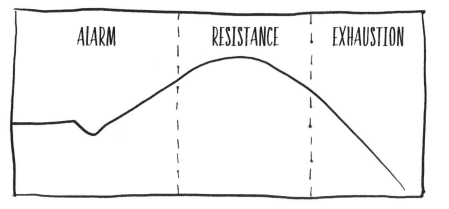

The three stages of the body's response to stress,
as described by Hans Seyle in 1946.

This diagram illustrates the three-stage response that the body has to stress, as first proposed by Hans Seyle in 1946. He called it the general adaptation syndrome, and described it as the body's way of adapting to a perceived threat to better equip it to survive. The three stages are:

1. Alarm reaction stage (fight/flight)
A distress signal is sent to a part of the brain. Stress hormones such as adrenaline and cortisol are released, boosting energy, and increasing heart rate and blood pressure as well as blood-sugar levels.

2. Resistance stage

The body tries to return things to normal by reducing stress hormones via the parasympathetic nervous system. If the stressful situation comes to an end, the body returns to normal. However, if this does not occur, the hormones continue to be produced, often resulting in the individual struggling to concentrate and becoming irritable.

3. Exhaustion stage

At this stage the body is no longer equipped to fight. This results in tiredness, depression, anxiety and feeling unable to cope, in the long term creating vulnerability to stress-related health conditions.

What becomes very clear from Seyle's pioneering research is that we are not designed to live in a constantly overstimulated and anxious state. As mentioned above, the body becomes exhausted, and anxiety and depression are probable outcomes. Hence it is highly likely that anxiety creates a neurological pathway into depression.

It is my view that they are without doubt 'unhealthy bedfellows'.

I also suspect, with some certainty, that anxiety is at the base of many suicides. In our youth, and in adults for that matter, I hypothesise that anxiety, mixed with a bit of substance abuse, is a perfect combo for suicide.

The last thing I have observed is the part anxiety plays in all of the major psychiatric disorders, such as schizophrenia and bipolar (manic depression).

The onset of relapse is so often a result of stress-related anxiety. I know this not only from clinical work but also from my own experience of having manic depression. When I look back on my episodes, each and every one was instigated by anxiety. Carl Jung theorised that mania was a defence against depression, and I agree—rather than feel sad and experience grief, I would wind up and continue with the mania, and then crash.

I hope you have found this guided
tour of the world of anxiety
both helpful and informative.
Remember, if you identify strongly
with any of these conditions,
please seek professional help.

PART 2

SOCIAL ANXIETY:

THE FEAR OF JUDGEMENT

CHAPTER
TEN

WHAT IS
SOCIAL
ANXIETY?

I would like now to introduce you to social anxiety, AKA the fear of judgement. I will take you through this very common phobia in more detail, as it is much overlooked and underdiagnosed, with individuals often not aware that what they are experiencing has a name and can be treated.

Note: The treatment approach discussed here—cognitive behavioural therapy (CBT)—is utilised effectively across the spectrum of anxiety conditions.

WHAT IS THE FEAR OF JUDGEMENT? A SYNOPSIS

The fear of being judged is a powerful and crippling phobia, underdiagnosed and misunderstood not only by health professionals, but also by the people who suffer every day as a result of this condition. What I mean by that is that people who live with this condition often assume that other people are thinking exactly the same way they do—hence, it is perceived as 'just the way life is'.

However, the fact of the matter is that other people, unless they have social phobia, are *not* thinking in this manner. (More on that later.)

DEFINING SOCIAL ANXIETY

The current *Diagnostic and Statistical Manual of Mental Disorders* (DSM-5) defines it this way:

> *Social Phobia/Social Anxiety Disorder: A persistent fear of one or more social or performance situations in which the person is exposed to unfamiliar people or to possible scrutiny by others. The individual fears that he or she will act in a way (or show anxiety symptoms) that will be embarrassing and humiliating.*

I am not about to argue this definition from an academic point of view (although this continues behind the scenes), as it certainly addresses a number of the challenges of this disorder. However, I am going to *redefine* aspects of it so that it means more to you.

The DSM-5 definition addresses the **fear of social situations**, especially when mingling with unfamiliar people. This could be at a party, or it could be going to the bank. However, I find it somewhat misleading, in that people with social anxiety do go into social situations—they do attend conferences, they attend school assembly. So it is not the same as claustrophobia, for instance, where people react adversely to being in a confined space with too many people. The key is that while you are in the room with those unfamiliar people, **you fear that people are judging you**.

Quite simply put, the *perceived* fear—the phobia— is of **other people's eyes**.

I emphasise the word *perceived*, because the belief that you are being judged is an *assumption*—it is not based in evidence, nor is it based in fact. Hence, it is a **perception of threat**, not a reality-based life threat.

You believe you are being judged because you are being guided by your irrational thoughts (based on assumption). Your thoughts then create the feeling of being judged, and now, believing in your emotions, you have even more fictional evidence that you are *in fact* being judged.

When what is *actually* true is that the person in the room judging you is *you*.

EVOLUTIONAL THEORY— EXCLUSION

Here is an interesting take on the possible origins of social anxiety. A couple of researchers, Baumeister and Tice (among others), hypothesised in the early 1990s that one major cause of this anxiety is exclusion from social groups. They suggested that the fear of being excluded—for example, the threat of the breaking of social bonds—is deeply rooted and may even have some biological basis.

In my opinion there is a great deal of merit in this theory. As primates, we are social beings, we are pack animals. Harry Harlow's (1965) research into the importance of 'maternal contact' utilising baby rhesus monkeys showed the following:

> *Infant rhesus monkeys taken away from their mothers, separated from peers and raised in laboratory settings showed disturbed behaviour—staring blankly, circling their cages and engaging in self-mutilation.*

Likewise, when human infants cry out with separation anxiety, remaining distressed until their mother comes back, they are ensuring inclusion. Children who wish to sleep with their parents at night fear social exclusion—it is not behaviour driven by an overactive appetite (well, not for food anyway).

This research, I believe, provides us with a better understanding of the depth and severity of the psychic pain experienced by the individual with social anxiety, and hence the disabling nature of the fear. It is a *primal need* to feel loved and connected— it's up there with food and water.

I find that in today's world, social exclusion from groups is real and often deliberate (in the form of bullying). People can be excluded because they don't wear the 'right' clothes, don't talk about the subjects valued by the group, don't share the common opinions, don't listen to the 'right' music. Hence, individuals who choose to avoid groups of people do so to avoid the anticipated pain of rejection, criticism and exclusion.

DO YOU HAVE SOCIAL ANXIETY?

The following scale, by Leary (1983), is the one I use the most to see if someone is struggling with social anxiety. As you will note, the scale is entitled the *Brief Fear of Negative Evaluation Scale*—meaning the same as the fear of judgement.

See my comments on page 110 about scoring. While I find this a useful tool to assess whether someone might be experiencing social anxiety, bear in mind that most people feel some concern about how they are perceived by others. As always, talk to a professional if you're concerned.

Brief Fear of Negative Evaluation Scale

Read each of the following statements carefully and indicate how characteristic it is of you according to the following scale:

1 = Not at all characteristic of me

2 = Slightly characteristic of me

3 = Moderately characteristic of me

4 = Very characteristic of me

5 = Extremely characteristic of me

___ 1. I worry about what other people will think of me even when I know it doesn't make any difference.

___ 2. I am unconcerned even if I know people are forming an unfavourable impression of me.

___ 3. I am frequently afraid of other people noticing my shortcomings.

___ 4. I rarely worry about what kind of impression I am making on someone.

___ 5. I am afraid others will not approve of me.

___ 6. I am afraid that people will find fault with me.

___ 7. Other people's opinions of me do not bother me.

___ 8. When I am talking to someone, I worry about what they may be thinking about me.

___ 9. I am usually worried about what kind of impression I make.

___ 10. If I know someone is judging me, it has little effect on me.

___ 11. Sometimes I think I am too concerned with what other people think of me.

___ 12. I often worry that I will say or do the wrong things.

(From: Leary, M. R. (1983). 'A brief version of the Fear of Negative Evaluation Scale', *Personality and Social Psychology Bulletin*, **9**, 371–376.)

Scoring: As the scale suggests, a score of 4 or 5 on an item shows that this trait is either very characteristic or extremely characteristic of you. On the reversed items (2, 4, 7, 10) a score of 1 or 2 gives an affirmative score (meaning you are demonstrating this trait). The numbers are not totalled—the patterns of the scores will give you the diagnostic information.

I would like to take this opportunity to point out to you the number of items in this scale that include the word 'worry'—for example, 'I often worry that I will say or do the wrong things', 'I am usually worried about what kind of impression I make', 'When I am talking to someone, I worry about what they may be thinking of me'.

Worry or worrisome overthinking coexists with social anxiety. However, unlike generalised anxiety, the worry is **specific to being judged by other people**. Hence, when it comes to the method of treatment—cognitive behavioural therapy (CBT)—the approach is able to address both worrisome overthinking and the fear of being judged *in unison*.

CHAPTER ELEVEN

MORE ON SOCIAL ANXIETY

The diagram opposite shows the model for cognitive behavioural therapy (CBT), which is recognised as the psychologically based therapy that is making the most significant contribution to the treatment of all anxiety and mood disorders, including social anxiety (the fear of being judged). I am going to utilise this model as a vehicle to explain to you the rest of the theoretical understanding on the possible origins of social anxiety disorder.

Back in the old days (the 1970s), we used to talk about nature versus nurture. As you can see in the model, contemporary scientific understanding links together all of the different components of being human: biology, behaviour, emotion and cognition (thought)—a bit like they did in the *really* old days.

Indulge me and have a read of this—it's very interesting!

In the CBT model, our biology, behaviour, emotion and cognition (thought) are inextricably linked.

THE MIND-BODY CONNECTION IN ANCIENT MEDICINE

The caduceus, the Western symbol of health and healing, has its origins in Ancient Greece. This well-known medical symbol depicts two snakes curled around the staff of the Greek god Hermes.

Each snake represents one of the two essential aspects of medicine. The outer aspect is our **biology**. The inner aspect is consciousness—our mental and spiritual life (**cognitive/emotional**).

We also take from the Ancient Greeks the word 'psychosomatic', meaning mind (psyche) and body (soma) working *in unison*, as they do (not separately). When applied to illness, the word psychosomatic has often offended people, as they believe it implies that they are just inventing their pain to get attention, when it actually means:

relating to or involving, or concerned with bodily symptoms caused by mental or emotional disturbance
—Merriam-Webster online dictionary

The Medicine Buddha is an Eastern symbol of health and healing. The wise figure of the Buddha is in a sitting position, holding a branch of the arura plant in his right hand, which symbolises all external therapeutic approaches to healing (**biological**). In his left hand, he holds a bowl containing the elixir of wisdom, the inner force of healing (**cognitive/emotional**).

These ancient symbols, arising from the human psyche across time and diverse cultures, are identical in meaning. They offer a universal wisdom gained by the great healers and sages of the past.

Amazing how far backward we managed to go— but the time when this knowledge was forgotten and

put aside wasn't called the Dark Ages for nothing!

Call me old-fashioned, but I have never seen the human world as being dictated by one element or another, or one aspect being dominant over the other. I have always believed in the inseparable relationship between biology and thought. (But then, I have never been a 'cure-grabber' either—I leave that to the narcissistic, egotistical, 'money-grabbers' among us, of which there is no shortage, it would appear.)

ENVIRONMENTAL CONTRIBUTORS

Before we go too much further, I want to mention a few of the pervasive environmental factors that come to play in the formation of social anxiety. (Note that with the CBT model, all four components—behaviour, biology, thoughts and emotions—sit within the environmental circle.)

The new framework for understanding in psychology (and other forms of medicine) is no longer nature versus nurture. We now speak of **epigenetics** providing a framework for understanding how the **expression of genes** is influenced by experiences and the environment, to produce individual differences in behaviour, cognition, personality and mental health.

I see it as a given that there are many influences from our individual experiences of the world. However, with particular reference to social anxiety I want to outline a few of the more prevalent risk factors:

- growing up in a family where conflict, trauma or abuse are experienced
- substance abuse in the family, and being ashamed to bring friends home
- experiencing teasing, bullying, rejection, ridicule or humiliation at school.

Let's face it, it doesn't take much to get bullied these days—you only need to have red hair, wear glasses, have the 'wrong' skin colour, speak with a stutter, have large/small breasts, be too fat/too thin/too tall, and/or have an out-of-date phone and you're a potential target.

Bullying in this twenty-first century world has gone to a whole other level of destructiveness with cyberbullying. Not to say that all forms of bullying are not destructive, but—wow—now you can be humiliated and ridiculed and have it go viral. The whole school is only a push of a button away.

I love the internet—it helps me research, it keeps me in touch with the world and my loved ones. But then there is the dark side. Cyberbullying I place in the domain of evil. I know for a fact that it leads to depression, anxiety, PTSD and suicide in our youth.

A note on social media

Often when I am interviewed by the media they want me to attribute all youth mental-health problems to social media. These complex conditions cannot be reduced to one phenomenon—this is called 'reductionism'. In fact, for someone with a fear of being judged the relationship with social media is multi-faceted.

For the individual with social anxiety, the use of social media can be a way to avoid phone or face-to-face interaction—hence avoiding interactions where they believe they won't come across well, and others will then evaluate them negatively. No one can see them blushing or perspiring, so they don't have to worry about that. They don't have to be anxious about stuttering when they send a text. A bit of a gift, it would appear—but in reality a temporary Band-Aid. Social media hence becomes a way of hiding their 'true self'.

Another phenomenon among the socially anxious are the 'passive users' of social media—people who observe but never participate by expressing opinions or posting on Facebook or Instagram. However, this position often results in constant comparison to others who are active on social media. The lives of other people are seen as so much more fun and perfect; others seem to be so much more popular. This is often accompanied by FOMO—the 'fear of missing out'—enhancing feelings of loneliness, isolation and undesirability.

A lot of my younger clients describe exactly this. They try to engage with social media and then risk more feelings of not being good enough to belong to the 'A Team' social group. It's almost as though you're damned if you do and damned if you don't.

INTROVERTED, EXTROVERTED— OR AM I JUST SHY?

If you are an introvert, you are someone who is energised and 'refuelled' by being by yourself or with a small group of loved ones. Your batteries are charged by alone time, unlike those of us who are born extroverts (such as myself), who feel there is nothing more relaxing after a hard week than having a bunch of mates around for burgers. Whether you are an introvert or an extrovert, you were born this way—it's a **trait**, or part of your inborn personality. Hence introverts make a choice—albeit a genetically predetermined one—to have plenty of alone time.

I have a number of introverted girlfriends, and I have learned a lot from them over the years—mostly, much to my horror, that they don't actually want to be like me! Their introverted behaviour is deliberate, and they have no aspiration to act otherwise. My darling girlfriend Jennifer sent me a cartoon similar to the one on the following page that explains it beautifully.

The best way to scientifically understand the difference between introverts and extroverts is via the differences in brain chemistry. We have three key chemicals in our brain:

- **dopamine**, the 'feel-good' chemical. When we engage in certain behaviours, such as socialising, more dopamine is released.
- **adrenaline**, which is activated by risk-taking, novelty (new things) and physical and environmental stimulation.
- **acetylcholine**, which is also linked to pleasure, but its effects are much more subtle.

The introvert *biologically* does not want to be overstimulated by dopamine. The extrovert, on the other hand, can't get enough of it.

> *Extroverts have more dopamine receptors in their brain, so they require more dopamine to feel happy, because they are less sensitive to it.*

> *In contrast, introverts are sensitive to dopamine, so all that stimulation makes them feel overwhelmed.*

Acetylcholine makes us feel relaxed, alert and content. It also fuels our ability to think deeply, reflect and focus for long periods of time on one thing. When we engage in activities that are low-key, calming and mentally engaging, we activate the release of acetylcholine.

While the introvert craves acetylcholine, the extrovert finds it a bit of a non-event—like a single gin and tonic in a tall glass. While those extroverts are out and about enjoying the benefits of all those extra dopamine receptors, introverts are happily lounging at home with a book and a pleasant dose of acetylcholine.

Yet again, the answer to so many of our questions on human behaviour is found in brain chemistry!

I want to comment, before we leave this discussion, on how much I object to the pressure in today's first-world culture to be an extrovert, as though extroversion is the ideal state of being. This is an arrogant assumption that minimises the equally valuable contribution made by introverts to all forms of decision-making, social change, the arts, and so on. Too often the extroverts attract attention because they are loud and talkative and hence seem more 'onto it'. But do they leave room to listen to others and deeply consider the issues at hand?

In my clinical practice I make it very clear to clients that the goal of therapy is not to become an extrovert (those individuals who are often envied) but **just to be comfortable in your own skin**.

SHYNESS AND SOCIAL ANXIETY

In my experience, we tend to talk of 'shyness' mostly in reference to children. Often adults will describe shyness as a phase the child is going through, and often it is just that. Most socially reserved children do grow into socially confident adults.

However, research shows us that childhood shyness *does* introduce an elevated risk of a person suffering social anxiety later in life (estimated to be between 30 and 40 per cent). Scientists define shyness as 'behavioural inhibition'—which is not the same as the introverted kids who just *like* spending time alone. The inhibited/shy kids *want* to interact but find it overwhelming.

Of course, this does not mean that all shy kids will develop social anxiety, but there is a significant link. The commonality in my mind is the part played by anxiety, fear and the feeling of being overwhelmed. It is perhaps best viewed as a spectrum, where shyness can be perceived as an early manifestation of social anxiety—remembering that this is not an absolute.

CHAPTER
TWELVE

THE
BIOLOGY
OF SOCIAL
ANXIETY

The diagram opposite gives you a picture of the different domains in which symptoms of social anxiety manifest themselves: physical/biological, behavioural and cognitive (thoughts).

Let's start with the biological side . . .

The genetic component or **heritability** of social anxiety is estimated to sit at around 30-40 per cent. This refers to the genetic predisposition—the prevalence running through the familial generations.

There is still a great deal about genes and anxiety that we do not know. However, a common theme across all of the anxiety disorders is **state anxiety**.

State anxiety is the experience of unpleasant emotional arousal in the face of threatening demands or danger.

For many people this experience is transitional and subsides in a relatively short period of time—anxiety is our alarm system, after all.

An individual with a genetic predisposition to 'high-trait' anxiety, on the other hand, will experience a more intense degree of state anxiety, with each incident taking longer to resolve.

Let me clarify this through the use of illustration. I want you to imagine that we measure how anxious and distressed people are feeling with a mood thermometer. Let's call it a mood-o-meter.

SUBJECTIVE UNITS OF DISTRESS (SUD)
Example: An anxious person

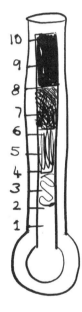

10 — 'I am dying' level panic

9

8 — 'Can't breathe' level panic

7 — Full-blown anxiety attack

6

5 — Sweaty palms, shallow breath

4

3 — Nervous and fidgety

2

1 — A bit tense, but OK

No feelings of distress

The mood-o-meter.

OK, now I want you to imagine two mood-o-meters, one for you with high-trait anxiety, and one for your bestie, who doesn't have that genetic predisposition.

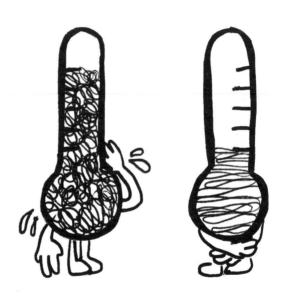

You both get startled by something—but look at how your buddy isn't really that fazed. You will also take longer to settle down, and will remember the experience as highly unpleasant.

Within this context, your emotional and biological memories are stored. You will remember the event as being *catastrophically* unpleasant. Hence, over time, any situations that result in an anxiety response, such as social gatherings, will be avoided. This behaviour becomes a way to avoid experiencing the anticipated anxiety, embarrassment and awkwardness that *may or may not occur*.

BIOLOGICAL SYMPTOMS

The following is a list of the types of symptoms that commonly occur with social anxiety:

- increased heart rate
- a sensation of the mind going blank
- upset stomach or nausea
- dizziness or lightheadedness
- muscle tension
- trembling.

These physical sensations are what accompany the switching-on of the fight/flight/freeze survival mechanism.

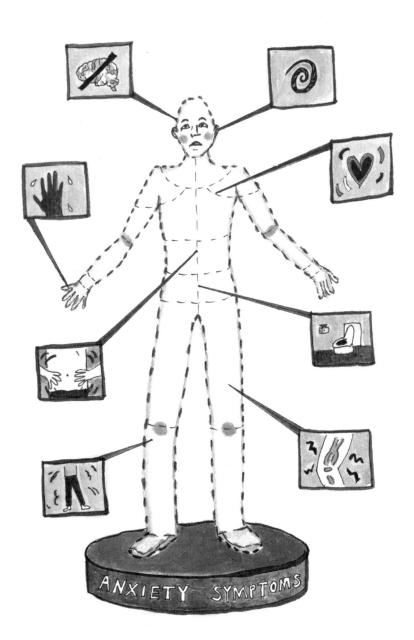

ANXIETY SYMPTOMS

There are two other sensations that I want to highlight, as they're often triggered by social anxiety.

Blushing

There is a specific 'fear of blushing' phobia—erythrophobia. The individual with social anxiety may not have this specific phobia, but may interpret blushing as a sign to others that they are embarrassed. They worry this could be perceived as a weakness, or social ineptitude. The fear of blushing is such a common manifestation of social anxiety that there are self-help books with titles such as *Dying of Embarrassment* (Barbara Markway, Alec Pollard, Teresa Flynn and Cheryl Carmin, 1992).

Like so many phenomena in the world of anxiety, this can become a self-perpetuating phobia, very similar to panic disorder—in that, the more you worry about blushing, the more you increase the probability of continuing to blush, and therefore reactivate the fear and shame you have associated with the blush.

Sweating

In the fight/flight/freeze response, the nervous system releases hormones, including adrenaline, which activate the sweat glands. This is a very natural biological response. However, if you have social anxiety, you are likely to interpret any tell-tale signs of sweating, such as damp armpits or damp shadows on clothing, as signs of weakness and social incompetence.

This is a different scenario to hyperhidrosis, which is abnormally excessive sweating usually affecting the hands, feet, underarms or face. This is a condition best treated medically. However, it has been my experience that some people can develop a degree of social anxiety as a result of this condition also.

These physical experiences are not life-threatening, abnormal or in any way dangerous. It is the *interpretation and meaning* given to these experiences that cause the distress (as you will learn about in the chapters to come).

CHAPTER THIRTEEN

SOCIAL ANXIETY AND BEHAVIOUR

Situations that can trigger social anxiety include:

- meeting people, including strangers
- talking in meetings or in groups
- starting conversations
- talking to authority figures
- working, eating or drinking while being observed
- going to school, shopping, being seen in public
- using public toilets
- public performance, including public speaking.

But, as I have mentioned, it is not that people who suffer from social anxiety don't attempt to do any of the above, especially if these are requirements of their work environment. It has to do with the discomfort and anxiety that they experience in the situation and *in anticipation* of such situations.

However, **avoidance** is undoubtedly the most prevalent of the behavioural patterns of social anxiety. Rather than experience social awkwardness, embarrassment or possible humiliation, the socially anxious person puts effort into avoiding situations when they fear their anxiety will be triggered. While they might be able to force themselves through uncomfortable situations at work, in their private social lives, where they have more control, they may, for example, convince their loved ones that they are too tired to go out, or are experiencing some minor physical ailment such as a headache or nausea. These strategies are also often utilised by people who are afraid they will be expected to speak in public, or who fear becoming the centre of attention at a social event, or who are afraid they might not know anyone at a party or function they have been invited to.

SAFETY BEHAVIOURS

Avoidance is known as a **safety behaviour**. As the thought of attending the event heightens your anxiety—anxiety in anticipation—the easiest way to remove this discomfort is to not attend. Then you can experience feeling safe at home, with no sensations of anxiety.

This approach does not come without its

complications, however, as your partner or other family members express their disappointment and frustration. Even so, this potential conflict and discontent does not tend to outweigh the fear of attending the event.

There are other safety behaviours that social anxiety sufferers employ:

Avoiding eye contact

People who suffer from a fear of judgement often have immense difficulty looking into other people's eyes. Avoiding eye contact is another strategy to reduce the anxiety. In my clinical work, observing rapid eye movement, with the client's eyes flicking from side to side, often serves as my first clue to a diagnosis.

Planning an exit

This might include knowing where the doors are and standing close to them, or standing with your back to the wall so you can see everyone in the room. Another tactic is making sure you can access your car keys, even in a chaotic and overfilled handbag.

Alcohol

One of the few ways the fight/flight/freeze mechanism can be numbed is through the use of alcohol. (Some people find marijuana provides the same effect.) Here's how it goes: you can't seem to get out of going to the party, so you do a bit of 'pre-loading' with a few drinks before leaving. This makes you more comfortable upon arriving. Then you have a few more and a few more to manage at the party.

Some people with social anxiety do not like the sensation of being affected by alcohol, as they much prefer to be in control. However, alcohol does serve as a nervous-system depressant, and hence will to a certain extent suppress the fight/flight sensations.

Party drugs

The bulk of the party drugs available these days have some form of amphetamine in the mix, hence they operate as stimulants. These include:

- cocaine (coke, Charlie)
- amphetamines (speed)
- methamphetamines (ICE, crystal meth, P)

- hallucinogens, including LSD (acid) and MDMA (ecstasy, E).

This last group is probably the most popular, and is often the drug of choice in rave and dance culture, and at festivals and house parties. They are also considerably cheaper than cocaine.

These are also very appealing substances for the socially anxious. They create an increased feeling of wellbeing, increased energy, decreased anxiety, and a feeling of emotional warmth and empathy. They achieve this by causing a greater release of serotonin and norepinephrine in the brain than is usually released. For example, the excess release of serotonin by MDMA is what causes the mood elevation.

However, the payback is that after the party weekend, serotonin levels in the brain are depleted and your mood drops. This comedown is often referred to as Ecky Tuesday.

This phenomenon hits the socially anxious hard. Because of their ever-present anxiety, their mood struggles to stay afloat.

It's totally understandable why such stimulants

would be attractive to the socially anxious, offering such a disinhibited utopia where they can finally feel part of the group. But messing with the receptors in charge of mood will have a cost attached.

THE PROBLEM WITH SAFETY BEHAVIOURS

The main issue with the safety behaviours is that they maintain the belief that the **perceived** danger is in fact real. Let me give you an example.

You have social anxiety, and you convince yourself that going to a street barbecue is going to be highly stressful—people will be judging you, and you will appear awkward, dull and boring. All of this has been created by your own thoughts and imagination. So you find a way to get out of going, feel better—and further reinforce the fear of such gatherings.

The model shown on the following page illustrates this process. You get the invite and then evaluate the whole experience negatively: 'I will be judged. People will think I'm boring. No one will want to talk to me.'

SOCIAL ANXIETY MODEL

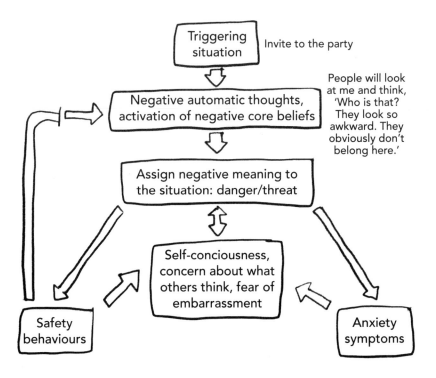

As a result of these beliefs, you begin to feel anxious. So you choose not to go—thereby avoiding the feelings of anxiety, but still maintaining the belief that going is dangerous.

Safety behaviours are common across a number of the anxiety conditions. Individuals with OCD might avoid cracks in the footpath, for example, in the fear that something bad will happen if they stand on the crack. The supermarket-phobic (who can of course now order online) clutches their trolley in terror, fearful of having an anxiety attack if they let it go. The chronic worrier must keep worrying to make sure nothing bad happens.

These are all superstitious behaviours, but the problem for the anxious is that, while they believe safety behaviours protect them, they fail to realise that the only thing they are protecting themselves from is their own self-generated anxiety. Hence, for them the beliefs far outweigh the facts.

ALCOHOL AS A SAFETY BEHAVIOUR

You have been invited to your partner's sister's engagement party. Trying to get out of this one

could result in a major falling-out. So to deal with the anticipatory anxiety (anxiety in anticipation of a perceived disaster), you have a few relaxing drinks before leaving.

You get to the party, and it's full of people you have never met before. You feel like hiding in a corner but don't, once again out of fear of enraging your partner.

So you grab a few more alcoholic beverages, and why not a few more? Next thing . . . you're the life and soul of the party!

Cracking jokes, dancing on the tables . . . No more social anxiety, you're a social dynamo—until the next day.

There's a big price to pay when you indulge to the point of oblivion. This is known as . . .

POST-MORTEM ANXIETY

This is a very common phenomenon with the fear of judgement. In some ways it is a unique element. It involves an excessively critical analysis of the social situation *after it has occurred*. For instance:

Oh no! I can't believe I did that in front of my boss's wife. She must think I am a complete loser. She's bound to talk to her husband, and he will think I'm a total liability and then I will lose my job, and I'll never get another job and my life will be ruined.

These post-mortems are more often than not based in your negative beliefs and attitudes and self-evaluation—rather than in facts. It is this collateral fallout and the debilitating post-mortem blues that discourage many of the socially anxious from drinking too much.

OTHER BEHAVIOURAL CHARACTERISTICS

Here are some other behavioural characteristics of the socially anxious.

Non-assertiveness

I always start therapy with a fairly extensive psychosocial questionnaire. This saves a lot of time with Q and A, and provides an excellent road map for the treatment plan. Individuals are asked to circle items that apply to them. Approximately 100 per cent of the time 'unassertive' is circled by the socially anxious.

The reason why? Well, to mix a few old adages, rather than 'put your foot in your mouth' and cause yourself a whole lot of embarrassment, it's better to take the safe road and say nothing. For those with a fear of judgement, saying nothing is the preferred option, even when they may have a differing opinion, or even if they want to make a request for a promotion or pay increase.

A very simple example, and very common one, is feeling discomfort to the point of inability to make a complaint at a restaurant or return food. The fear of being judged, angering the restaurant staff or feeling embarrassed becomes more overwhelming than the cost of being ripped off.

Handwriting

This may seem a little odd, but in my clinical practice I am never surprised to see tiny handwriting by people with social anxiety. Clients will often say things like, 'Sorry, my handwriting is terrible.'

I have hypothesised a couple of reasons for this phenomenon:

- feeling discomfort at writing in front of someone (for example, a bank teller)
- fearing their style of writing is being judged.

I have also wondered if there is a connection between dyslexia and social anxiety. The reason I say this is that dyslexia is often circled on the aforementioned questionnaire by those with social anxiety, particularly by my more mature clients.

For a long time dyslexia was not diagnosed or accounted for in classrooms as it is today. Hence pupils may have been asked to write something on the blackboard and experienced great discomfort and humiliation if/when the classroom erupted in laughter at the jumbled spelling.

PERFORMANCE, PERFECTIONISM, PROCRASTINATION AND CELEBRITY

erfectionism is an important belief and behavioural pattern for those with a fear of judgement, as clearly evidenced by the prevalence of sufferers of perfectionism and social anxiety disorder in the performing arts.

It seems counter-intuitive that people who make a living on screen or in front of large audiences can feel the extremes of this anxiety. But here's a small list I have compiled from the millions of entries on Google for 'celebrity perfectionists':

- Hugh Grant
- Oprah Winfrey
- Taylor Swift
- Adele
- Stephen Colbert
- Prince, who has been described as a shy, awkward figure. After his death, people he had worked with also spoke of his relentless perfectionism. Opioids—as well as treating the chronic pain they

had been prescribed for—were of course ideal for sedating his self-critical mind-chatter.

- Johnny Depp, who has been very open about his struggle with social anxiety.

Actors or entertainers get to play another person, live another life, be someone else, and so it is their role/performance being judged and evaluated, not themselves. As long as the performance is perfect, they can manage. It is often when they are being interviewed and are speaking as their 'true selves' that they are more likely to become anxious.

Barbra Streisand, another phenomenal talent, stopped singing live for almost thirty years as a result of her anxiety. She described it this way: during a performance in New York City's Central Park in 1967, she forgot the lyrics to a song while performing. It is this incident that she considers the beginning of her social phobia. Another extreme perfectionist, she could neither forgive herself nor find the courage to get back on the stage and sing. She lived in fear of forgetting the words again, and returned to live performance only with the use of a teleprompter, so she would not have to worry.

In these personal accounts, the fear of being judged is shifted away from the self, via perfect performance. Hence the performance, not the self, is evaluated. Musicians can achieve this by creating an effective mask with the use of their instrument, hiding behind the sound. Again, the performance via the instrument is evaluated, not their person. This is why they place such emphasis on perfectionism in terms of their performance.

If you're a perfectionist, you may find this maxim helpful:

In his book *Too Perfect: When Being in Control Gets Out of Control*, Dr Allan Mallinger unpacks perfectionism into two different camps: positive and negative.

POSITIVE PERFECTIONISM

These individuals aspire to excellence; however, they are not driven by a fear of failure. They know when they have done their best, and are able to complete tasks without endless checking and rechecking into the small hours at the risk of burning out.

NEGATIVE PERFECTIONISM

According to psychologist Dr David Burns, this is where individual standards 'are high beyond reach or reason'. These people 'strain compulsively and unremittingly toward impossible goals and measure their worth entirely in terms of productivity and achievement'. They are highly self-critical and fearful of mistakes, and because of this are more prone to anxiety, depression, feeling inadequate, procrastination and shame.

PERFECTIONISM AND PROCRASTINATION

Entire books have been written on this cause-and-effect relationship. I will mention it only briefly here, because of the link between social anxiety and perfectionism discussed above. You see, when you live with a fear of being judged, one mechanism to attempt to avoid the discomfort of this belief is to strive, and strive, and strive for everything you do to be perfect (negative perfectionism). The unrelenting demands of this are exhausting, and situations like the following evolve . . .

You have a really important assignment to complete and it has to be 'perfect'. There is so much riding on its completion.

You approach your desk, only to notice it's in a bit of a mess. 'Mmmm . . . there's no way I can work under these conditions—better just do a quick tidy-up,' you decide.

Tidying the desk, doing all the filing from the last two years and colour-coding your pens takes forever. Time for a coffee break.

'Wow, is that the time?' you exclaim to yourself. 'May as well have lunch and get back into it this afternoon.'

You make your favourite soup and whip up a quick-to-make sourdough bread. As long as you finish lunch by about 1 p.m., all will be well. Back to the office.

'OK, now where was I? That's right, the topic: "The World in 2050: Will the shift in global economic power continue?"

'WTF am I supposed to do with that? I guess I'll have to do a bit of Googling. There's no way I'm going to tackle something that huge today!'

You Google:

'global': 4,400,000,000 results

'economic power': 1,470,000,000 results

'shift': 160,000,000 results

'No f@cking way am I going to get anywhere near this today. Looks like it will be an early start tomorrow. It has to be perfect.'

And so on . . .

And so it goes on, day after day, with the fear of an imperfect outcome inhibiting any attempts at actually beginning. However, with each delay the deadline is closing in.

A lot of procrastinators say to me: 'It doesn't bother me, I work my best with a tight deadline.' This is an interesting belief given that there is more anxiety closer to the deadline, so the brain's efficacy is then impaired by the biochemical changes.

What is true, however, is that procrastination does provide a reprieve from the perfectionistically induced anxiety and the fear of failure. However, the reprieve is only temporary, and in fact perpetuates the cycle.

THE CYCLES OF PROCRASTINATION

Perfectionism/Fear of Failure

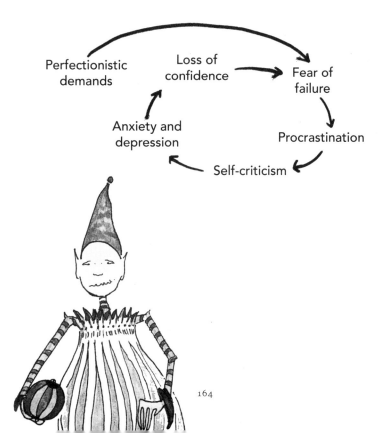

Perfectionistic demands → Loss of confidence → Fear of failure → Procrastination → Self-criticism → Anxiety and depression → (back to Perfectionistic demands)

Author indulgence

I have always found there is something quite nice about being in the company of talented people who also battle with mental illness. It seems to normalise it for people somehow. As someone with bipolar disorder, I get to share my diagnosis with:

- Russell Brand (comedian)
- Mariah Carey (singer)
- Winston Churchill (politician)
- Patricia Cornwell (writer)
- Patty Duke (actress)
- Stephen Fry (actor)
- Spike Milligan (comedian)
- Jackson Pollock (painter)
- Ruby Wax (actress)

The list goes on and on. Of course, this doesn't mean that everyone with a mental-health condition is a brilliant writer, actor, painter or composer, but there does appear to be a disproportionate number of troubled creatives. This suggests to me that the 'highly sensitive' tend to be highly sensitive to everything. Hence, this sensitivity acts as a curse and a gift all at the same time.

CHAPTER FIFTEEN

EMOTION AND THOUGHT

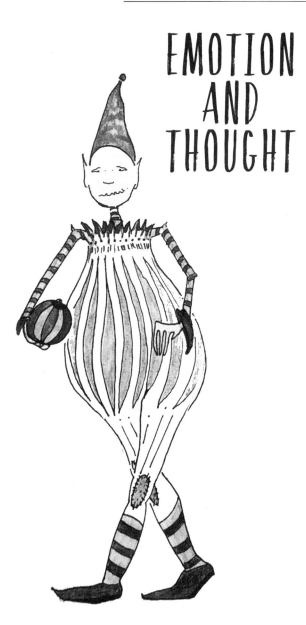

There are a range of emotions attached to the experience of social anxiety. The list below shows just a few of the common ones. I have a longer list that I have formulated as a result of the work I have done with clients over many years. It's an extensive and overpowering list, and I am sure I have forgotten a few!

FEAR
OF HUMILIATION
— EMBARRASMENT
SHAME
AWKWARDNESS
ISOLATION
ENVY

As illustrated, the overriding emotion is **fear**. The connecting point to the other emotions is worrisome overthinking (worry). It goes like this: you worry about being humiliated, you worry about becoming embarrassed, you worry about feeling awkward, and in the process of worrying about these events—that have not as yet happened—you start to experience fear and anxiety.

Note: Just to reiterate, worry is the common denominator across the Anxiety Family. For example, worrying about a plane crashing when you fly; worrying about being fat if you have anorexia; worrying about your sexual performance; and, if you have social anxiety, worrying about being judged.

When you send a message via the messenger of 'worrisome overthinking', you tell your amygdala that you are in actual danger. The **amygdala** is a group of neurons in your brain shaped like an almond—hence its name, which comes from the Greek word for almond. It is related to the processing of emotions, especially fear.

When the amygdala senses danger, in a split second the fight/flight/freeze response is activated. This occurs prior to any rational processing from the **neocortex** (the part of the brain responsible for reasoning, conscious thought, language, sensory perception, and so on).

The amygdala is the more primitive part of our brain. Without the capacity to reason and differentiate, it sends out the same evolutionary response to perceived threats (psychological) as it would to actual physical danger. Because of the phenomenal speed of this exchange, the amygdala essentially 'hijacks' the system.

If I were reincarnated as a brain, I would be highly pissed off about being stirred up by these constant false alarms!

Again, I would like to emphasise that the

predominant theme with social anxiety, in the emotional domain, is fear. With the other emotions—for example, shame, embarrassment, humiliation—it is the *fear* of these emotions being noticed by others and judged.

A number of the other emotional responses, such as frustration, irritability, despair and sadness, are the by-products of constantly living with fear and anxiety. Irritability and frustration are the result of not being able to escape from the constant negative mind-chatter.

Arrogance also comes under this classification. People with the fear of being judged are often described as arrogant by others. For example, 'Did you see that guy who just walked in? He didn't even say hello or make eye contact—talk about arrogant!' The funny thing is that the truth is quite the opposite.

There is a saying in Hindi:

अहंकार असुरक्षा का छलावा है

In English: Arrogance is the camouflage of insecurity.

Now for the most important bit . . .

THOUGHT

In the CBT model, as previously explained, thought is referred to as **cognition**—but let's keep it simple. For the most part we are talking about 'thought', not all of the other processes that sit under the umbrella of cognition (comprehension, knowing, remembering and problem-solving).

Returning to the basic CBT model, the most important thing to understand is that inextricable link between the four domains.

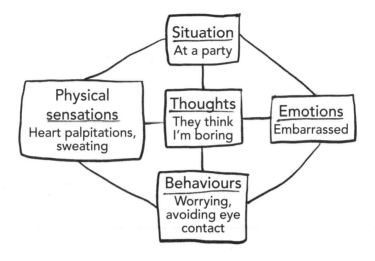

An external situation occurs, or maybe just a worrisome thought (internal trigger). Then the responses to the stimulus occur (at times hijacked by the amygdala). You experience physical (biological) sensations and emotions, and then you do things (behaviour).

The next step—which is really important for you to understand—is what the practical application of the model looks like, and how it works.

So this is how it goes:

A: There is an event (internal/external trigger).

B: You think about the event. But most importantly you give the event a *meaning*. It is not just the thought, but also *how* you think, how you evaluate the trigger, and the meaning that you give the event.

C: Once this has occurred—in a millisecond or thereabouts—the responses occur: physical, emotional, behavioural (for example, avoidance, worry and so on).

Note: Worrisome overthinking is categorised as a **behaviour** as it is something we **do**. (Refer to *The Book of Overthinking* for more information on worry as a behaviour and how worry is learned.)

MEDICATION AND
SOCIAL ANXIETY

This ABC model can be applied to the entirety of the Anxiety Family. But what is noteworthy with social phobia is the profound influence that specific **thinking errors** (more on these shortly) have on the style and content of a person's thoughts.

Many pharmaceutical companies have their medications registered for the treatment of social phobia, but these medications (SSRIs or selective serotonin reuptake inhibitors—see page 28) only help a little—they do *not* change the cognitive style. CBT leads the field with regards to effective, sustainable treatment.

I am not going to list all of the thinking styles of social phobia in isolation; I'm going to weave them in as examples as we go through the treatment method.

PART 3

THERAPY TIME

CHAPTER SIXTEEN

THERAPY SESSION ONE

Right, let's get started . . . it's therapy time!

Coming into my office is going to be a real challenge. You have probably spent quite a bit of time last night trying to think of ways to get out of turning up—tossing and turning, listening to mind-chatter that goes a little bit like this:

This is stupid.

I'm not crazy.

I don't need to go and talk to some stranger and get charged a whole lot of money.

I can get through this on my own.

What's she going to do anyway?

Probably just put me on medication, and there is no way I'm doing that!

So that thinking goes around and around . . . before you know it, it's time to get up: you have your first appointment.

Oh, why not? I may as well go. I don't have to go back, after all.

I come into the room and the first thing I take note of is where you are sitting and what you are doing while you wait. You're possibly leaning up against the wall near the front entrance, or sitting on the chair that's the most isolated from any others in the waiting room. You might be glued to your electronic device, probably with headphones plugged in—nice and safe from the outside world.

I wander over, shake your hand, lead you up to my office and point you towards a selection of two armchairs. Once we are seated, I ask you to introduce me to your story and what it is you would like some help with.

You do your best to avoid looking at me, pausing only occasionally to make direct eye contact (safety behaviour).

Looking directly into my eyes risks the possibility of being evaluated negatively. The irony is that you are actually *paying me* to evaluate you, but that piece of irony I usually leave until you know me a little better.

> **Me**: So tell me a bit about yourself and what it is that you would like me to help you with.

You provide me with some general information about your life and your living circumstances. When I ask for a more specific definition of your problem you struggle to find the words. A bit like this:

> **You**: I have a lot of sadness and self-doubt.
> **Me**: Do you think you're depressed?
> **You**: No, I think I would know if I was depressed. I mean, I know I am an introvert, but I just find it very difficult to mix with new people. Often my friends will ask me to go to things, but I always try to find a way not to go.
>
> I know my friends and family get frustrated with me, but even if I think about going I start to feel nauseous, my heart starts to beat fast and I get shaky. Then there's no way I feel like going, so I make some excuse and avoid going.
>
> Then the next thing is that I start feel guilty for not going, and find myself becoming irritable and snappy. Then I feel guilty because I have snapped at my friends and family.

By this stage I can hear more and more clues to the source of the discomfort, particularly physically (nausea, shakiness) and emotionally (fear, guilt, irritability).

Time to assess the anxiety more formally. I give you Leary's Brief Fear of Negative Evaluation Scale to fill out.

Brief Fear of Negative Evaluation Scale

Read each of the following statements carefully and indicate how characteristic it is of you according to the following scale:

1 = Not at all characteristic of me

2 = Slightly characteristic of me

3 = Moderately characteristic of me

4 = Very characteristic of me

5 = Extremely characteristic of me

(From: Leary, M. R. (1983). 'A brief version of the Fear of Negative Evaluation Scale', *Personality and Social Psychology Bulletin*, **9**, 371–376.)

5 1. I worry about what other people will think of me even when I know it doesn't make any difference.

1 2. I am unconcerned even if I know people are forming an unfavourable impression of me.

4 3. I am frequently afraid of other people noticing my shortcomings.

1 4. I rarely worry about what kind of impression I am making on someone.

5 5. I am afraid others will not approve of me.

1 6. I am afraid that people will find fault with me.

1 7. Other people's opinions of me do not bother me.

5 8. When I am talking to someone, I worry about what they may be thinking about me.

5 9. I am usually worried about what kind of impression I make.

1 10. If I know someone is judging me, it has little effect on me.

4 11. Sometimes I think I am too concerned with what other people think of me.

5 12. I often worry that I will say or do the wrong things.

Me: Looks like that really resonated for you.
You (sort of nervously): Sure did.
Me: This is a terrible burden to live with, don't you find?

Somewhat mystified, you glance at me and nod in acknowledgement.

Me: OK, well let me explain to you what is going on.

I explain the definition of social anxiety/phobia, highlighting the very close relationship it has with worrisome overthinking and the fear of judgement.

Me: These two thought patterns in particular are totally intertwined.

You see, people who suffer from worrisome overthinking essentially worry about everything (generalised anxiety). Whereas for you, your major concern is what other people are thinking about you, with the overriding assumption that whatever they are thinking will be negative and judgemental.

Hence, what you experience (subjectively) is that negative judgemental thoughts are directed at you from other people, wherever you are.

Your assumption goes like this:

> **Ninety-nine per cent of people, at any one time, in a room that I am in, are thinking about me.**

The truth is more like:

> **Ninety-nine per cent of the time, other people are thinking about themselves.**

Here's another common assumption:

> **One or more people in the room are thinking exactly the same negative stuff about me that I am thinking about myself, at the exact same time.**

The truth is more like:

> *I* am the one thinking that I am boring and dull, and then I project my thoughts (in a nanosecond) across to some unsuspecting random individual on the other side of the room.

Your every waking moment is lived in constant warfare with your own thoughts—endless negative mind-chatter.

Such mind-chatter is *not* just a harmless fact of life—far from it. It creates a great deal of your physical and emotional discomfort. It causes concentration difficulties, impairs memory, and interferes with productivity, creativity and intimacy. It is truly a curse.

This self-focused thinking provides you with the content for your perception of yourself, your confidence or lack of, your beliefs about your value as a person. It is also responsible for creating thinking habits and, like any other habit, the thoughts and beliefs become ingrained, and you start to experience them as true, even though:

Beliefs are *not* facts.

Before we go on, I want to tell you a social anxiety story with a happy ending.

Many years ago now, a lovely gentleman in his mid- to late sixties presented with post-operative depression after having a brain tumour removed. He was dressed all in grey, very plain and understated. Having observed his lack of direct eye contact, I administered the Brief Fear of Negative Evaluation Scale. His responses were affirmative and confirmed a diagnosis of social anxiety.

He was taking antidepressants, and while they had helped with his depression he was, in his words, 'only living half a life'.

After a course of CBT he blossomed. I will never forget his last session. He arrived in red jeans, a brightly coloured Hawaiian shirt and bright-blue sneakers. He was off to bungy-jump after our session.

Before he left he looked me straight in the eye and said: 'Gwendoline, my only regret was that I did not meet you when I was sixteen years old. I have half-lived my life hiding behind this condition, not knowing what it was, just accepting it as my lot in life. Thank you so much.'

Therein lies the reason I love my job—and for you the message is that no matter how old you are, you can be helped.

Moving right along . . . I hope you have found this first session educational and it has enhanced your awareness. Having a name for this weird experience is often incredibly liberating.

> **Finally, someone knows what this is that goes on in my head. It has a name and, of course, if it has a name, people must know how to fix it.**

And that is the truth of the matter. Out of every seven clients a day that I see, at least three present with the fear of judgement. It is very treatable, at all stages of life.

It's very OK to be hopeful!

HOMEWORK

The table shown opposite is called a thought record. This provides you with a template to record situations between now and when I see you next that have caused you distress.

This is how it works:

Thought record: Column A

This is where you describe the experience/incident that you want to discuss. It is important that you keep this description brief and factual. Be mindful of not including emotions and physical sensations in this description.

It will take you a little while to get used to separating thoughts and emotions, but don't be too concerned about this—it takes practice. You are describing the *reality*, also known as the event or trigger. As I mentioned earlier this can be an external event (for example, receiving an invitation to a party), or an internal trigger (for example, thinking about a job interview you have the following week).

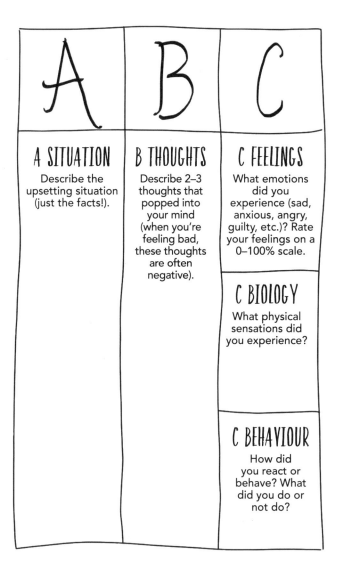

A	B	C
A SITUATION Describe the upsetting situation (just the facts!).	**B THOUGHTS** Describe 2–3 thoughts that popped into your mind (when you're feeling bad, these thoughts are often negative).	**C FEELINGS** What emotions did you experience (sad, anxious, angry, guilty, etc.)? Rate your feelings on a 0–100% scale. **C BIOLOGY** What physical sensations did you experience? **C BEHAVIOUR** How did you react or behave? What did you do or not do?

The thought record:
understanding the relationship between
thoughts, feelings and behaviour.

Thought record: Column B

This is where you record the thoughts that are occurring, racing through your mind. Try to grab as many of these thoughts as you can. Don't censor your recording. It is important that I have a full understanding of the content of your thoughts. I'm going to be the last person who thinks you're crazy, so just activate the download button!

These are called 'automatic thoughts' because they are the ones that you are conscious of and are spontaneous and free-flowing.

Thought record: Column C

These are your responses, in the three categories of **Feelings**, **Biology** and **Behaviour**. Because the sensations and feelings occur so quickly, you may find it helpful to record them first, before you enter the thoughts in column B, but I'll leave that up to you—it doesn't matter that much.

Just to refresh your memory:

Feelings are the emotions you experience. For example: fear, embarrassment, shame, anger, irritability.

Biology refers to the physical sensations you experience. For example: racing heart, shallow breathing, sweaty palms, knotting in your stomach, nausea.

Behaviour is anything that you do in response to the stimulus/trigger. For example: pacing, worrying, avoiding.

You will notice that in the Feelings column there is a requirement to rate how intense your experience is on a scale of 0–100 per cent. Back to the mood-o-meter.

We call this a **SUDS (Subjective Units of Distress Scale)** rating. This means I want you to rate the intensity of the emotion *as it occurs for you*. Don't attempt to rationalise this—it is important that I get to see what you experience, not what you *think* you should be experiencing.

For instance, you might start to think, *This is so ridiculous. I shouldn't be feeling this anxious just because I have to go into the bank. People go into the bank every day. I've been to the bank before and been OK.*

But writing down a score of 20 per cent because it 'looks better' is not helpful. The rating needs to be accurate, because it becomes a means of observing and measuring your progress during therapy.

There is one more thing I want to point out to you about the ABC model, as it will enhance your understanding of the therapeutic method.

A = reality

This is not the problem! Reality just is, and 'shit happens'.

C = responses to the trigger

These are defined as the problem. People just

like you come for therapy because they don't like what they are feeling emotionally/physically, and they don't like what they're having to do to keep comfortable and safe.

B = the intervention

This is where the therapy takes place. The thinking (B) creates the responses (C). Hence the changes need to occur in *how you think*. I cannot emphasise enough how important it is for you to not only understand this, but also believe it. 'Know how you think, change how you feel'—it was even used as the subtitle in the first book in this series.

Me: Well, that's enough brain food for today . . . just one more thing. Before you go, I want to introduce you to the use of breathing exercises.

Breathing

When you are feeling anxious, it can really help if you remember to breathe. That sounds a bit crazy, because we're always breathing, right? But what happens when you're anxious is that you can tend to hold your breath and this makes everything worse. When you feel like that, try this:

- hold your breath for six counts (don't make the mistake of taking a deep breath and hyperventilating, though)
- breathe out
- breathe in for three counts
- breathe out for three counts
- breathe in for three counts
- and so on . . .

The benefits of this little technique are impressive. You get the benefit of settling your biology (nervous)

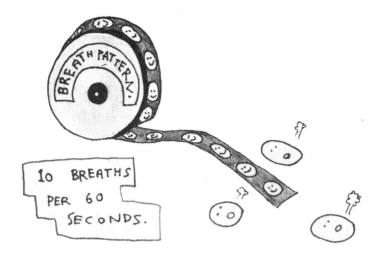

10 BREATHS PER 60 SECONDS.

system, as well as a cognitive distraction via the counting. The in-for-three, out-for-three counting system is based on our resting breathing pattern (ten breaths per sixty seconds). I give my clients a little set of stickers to put everywhere around them to remind them to do the exercise, like little prompts. I recommend doing it at least six times a day.

When you reach very high levels of distress, this exercise is not that potent. However, if you do it throughout the day, you can reduce your baseline level of anxiety. It is also helpful for when you are anticipating getting anxious before an event.

The other beauty of such a low-effort technique is that there is no excuse for not making the time! You can do it anywhere—you don't have to lie down, you don't have to listen to dolphin music.

The exercise is also invisible. Gentle breaths in and out, no deep breathing—hence, no concerns about people looking at you.

CHAPTER
SEVENTEEN

THERAPY SESSION TWO

Me: Hi, how have you been? What did you think about our first session?

You: Good. I was quite surprised how different I felt last week.

Me: In what way?

You: It just seemed to make such a difference actually finding out a few things about social anxiety. The fear of being judged made so much sense to me—that's just what it's like.

It didn't stop happening, but I was more aware of what was going on with my thinking and that it wasn't normal. You know what I mean? Other people aren't thinking like me all the time. I felt relief. It was like a lightbulb moment.

Me: That's great news. People often describe experiencing a bit of an epiphany, with a new awareness and the beginnings of a deeper insight.

The only thing I would like to say is that this awareness is only the beginning of this process. When you first have a label for what you go through, there is a bit of a honeymoon period of 'feeling good'. I'm not meaning to put a dampener on this for you; however, it is doing the work and learning the skills and techniques that will maintain this new sense of feeling good.

There is another chunk of knowledge you will need, and this is the educational content of today's session. I need you to digest this information as we go along, as this knowledge becomes an integral part of therapy and subsequent change, so bear with me.

To keep things simple and easy to understand, I like to use the metaphor of a computer to describe some of the functions of the brain, in relation to the CBT model.

Just going back a moment to the ABC model, I mentioned to you last week that the therapeutic intervention occurs in column B, because it is the evaluation of the trigger (via your thinking) that will determine how you feel and respond. It is the *meaning* you give the event that will trigger your fight/flight response, particularly if you label the trigger as dangerous and to be feared.

I want you to imagine that you enter your thoughts into your computer (the metaphorical brain). The thoughts input through the software system, and then, through a relationship with the hard drive, an output is created.

Let me explain for you in therapeutic terms ...

COMPUTER-BRAIN ANALOGY: A COGNITIVE THERAPY PERSPECTIVE

1. You have a hard drive, where all your core beliefs and values are stored from way back when. This includes your early life history, your role-modelling, your value system.

Although not in keeping with the purest form of the model, I also include genetic predisposition (high-trait anxiety) in this metaphor.

2. Then there is the software package, where your rules of living and your attitudes are stored. These rules often present in your thinking as the 'if-thens'. (As you are learning about the world as a child, you observe that if you behave in one way you see a desirable outcome, and if you behave differently the outcome is not so good, and you learn to choose the behaviour that works in your home. This establishes rules of behaviour and how things 'should' be in order for you to adapt and survive.)

3. The screen. This is where the thoughts that you are conscious of in your daily life are displayed. Here we are focusing on the negative automatic thoughts, as these are the ones causing the trouble.

Sounds straightforward, and so it would be if the mind didn't play tricks with your perception of reality. There are certain learned ways of thinking that really do cause havoc in the processing and meaning-giving systems.

These tricks of the mind can cause significant distortions for you when evaluating your world. I'm going to introduce them to you in some detail. Once again, I can't emphasise enough the importance of becoming very familiar with these thought distortions/thinking errors, as recognising them at work is vital to the success of the therapy.

There are certain aspects of cognitive therapy that are like learning to speak a foreign language. Most sciences have a 'jargon' unique to them, and cognitive science is no exception.

TRICKS OF THE MIND— THOUGHT DISTORTIONS

There are a number of cognitive distortions (AKA thinking errors). I am going to list them all here for you. However, I will focus in more detail on those that cause the most confusion when negotiating reality through the 'fear of being judged' lens.

Get to know the common thought distortions (thinking errors), so that you can identify when your mind is playing tricks on you.

All-or-nothing thinking

Often described as 'black-and-white thinking'. This is a very rigid and extreme way of appraising the world, which as we know is mostly grey. People who engage in this form of thinking use words like always/never, nobody/everybody, everything/nothing.

This style of thinking is common with depression, adding to the perceived hopelessness of life—a life that will never be any better and will always be a frightening, dark struggle. It is also common for people who have experienced trauma or people who experience anxiety in a social situation. When your fight/flight/freeze mechanism is switched on, your thinking is polarised. Fight/flight = black/white. As I have mentioned before, when the amygdala is activated there is no reasoning or abstract reasoning—it is about your survival.

Overgeneralisation

Another extreme way of thinking, usually with a strong pessimistic flavour. *One* negative outcome is perceived as a predictor of what is to occur throughout life, one disaster after another. Not much to look forward to there!

Negative mental filter

Cognitive theorists often use the analogy of constantly wearing a pair of shit-coated glasses.

The negative filter is a classic illustration of this phenomenon.

If you view the world through these 'shit-coated lenses', before too long you are going to believe that the world is a shitty place to be. Depressives, pessimists and worrisome overthinkers see the world in this way.

The assumption when you have a fear of judgement is that other people will evaluate you negatively, and this works in unison with your constant theme of negative self-evaluation.

Disqualifying the positive

This distortion has a double-whammy impact on your perception. You maintain the negative mental filter, and at the same time you negate any positive outcome you may achieve.

People often talk about the 'imposter syndrome' through this lens. For example: 'I don't know how I got this job—there are so many people better than me. One day someone will turn up and realise I am not good enough, and I will be exposed as an imposter.'

This constant self-downing is how your lack of confidence and your negative self-beliefs are reinforced and hence maintained.

Labelling

You decide you have committed some social *faux pas* (French for f@ck-up) at a work do. Not only do you focus on the event, but then you also label yourself a complete idiot and a loser. Bit strong for having made a simple mistake, but that is what your phobia leads you to believe.

Magnification (AKA catastrophising)

The old saying for these rather long words goes like this: Don't make a mountain out of a molehill.

For example, you rally up all your courage at a dinner party—of course, full of people you believe to be so much more witty and intelligent than yourself—and decide to tell a joke. A collection of people laugh, but there are others who don't. You, of course, assume that this is because you're an idiot, not taking into account that they may have

been focused elsewhere and didn't even know you were telling a joke.

When you apply your magnification lens, everything becomes exaggerated, and the more you exaggerate the worse you feel.

Your self-talk goes something like this:

'I can't believe I just did that. That is the worst possible thing I could ever have done. This will be remembered forever. I will never live it down!'

Notice how the all-or-nothing thinking distortion steps in to really create that sensation of an overwhelming catastrophe.

I can't stand it-itis

After something has been hugely catastrophised, it then of course becomes catastrophically overwhelming. You then start telling yourself that you cannot be in the situation anymore, that it is unbearable and that you are not going to cope, because this is the worst thing that has ever happened to you.

Once you start thinking in this way, your fight/flight mechanism is switched on and you are being prepared to do just that: fight or run. With the adrenaline now going through your system you will of course become increasingly uncomfortable, reinforcing this belief that you cannot and will not ever be able to tolerate these situations.

In fact, you have lived successfully through far more difficult situations. Hence, telling yourself you 'can't stand it' is not true.

Minimisation

This is the opposite of magnification and a close cousin to disqualifying the positive. Instead of making a mountain out of a molehill, you take the mountains and shrink them into tiny molehills. Hence, you never take any credit, embrace your successes or enjoy the moment.

Jumping to conclusions

The strongest element of the jumping-to-conclusions cognitive style is the total reliance on assumption to negotiate the real world. Facts are discarded and replaced by unsubstantiated beliefs and emotions. This is a good time to remind you that:

Beliefs are not facts.
Feelings are not facts either.

There are two thought distortions that operate in this realm: mind-reading and fortune-telling.

Mind-reading

Also based totally on assumption, you convince yourself that you can read other people's minds. Hand in hand with that is the belief that they can also read your mind, leaving you feeling vulnerable and transparent.

Of course you would believe that they can read your mind, because while you are reading their mind, they must be reading yours. The assumption is that we all think alike, so we are all mind-readers.

The truth is, however, that all those thoughts that you perceive to be transmitted from other people's minds are thoughts that originate and exist *only in your mind*. This is called **projection**.

Anna Freud (Sigmund's daughter, for those of you who remember the pioneer of psychoanalysis) described projection as a **psychological defence**

mechanism, through which an individual attributes unwanted thoughts, feelings and motives to another person. This creates a powerful illusion of mirrors, reflected thoughts and the strong emotions of rejection and exclusion.

A belief in 'mind-reading' is a perfect example of the unknown deception of the thinking errors. You are not consciously aware that you are mind-reading. You probably describe yourself as 'being very intuitive and good at reading people'.

The flaws of these beliefs often do not become real for people until they begin therapy.

False belief:

The belief that people are thinking about you, when the majority of the time they are thinking about themselves—

just like you are.

False belief:

The belief that people are
thinking exactly the same
negative things about you that
you're thinking at exactly the
same time—now that's spooky!

Fortune-telling

This is part two of the 'jumping to conclusions'
thought distortion—where you are able to predict
the future. OK, you may not be able to predict the
lottery numbers, but this distortion convinces you
that you know what people will be thinking about
you *in the future*. It goes like this . . .

> Anyway, there I was trying to stay below the
> radar after having told the worst joke of my
> life. There was this woman at the far end of
> the table and she looked at me. I just knew
> she was thinking, 'What an idiot.'

So you have read her mind, and then forecasted
what she will think and say to the host in the future.

This is clearly not possible, but you believe it. You may even plan a way to seek reassurance from the host, to try to alleviate your anxiety, or at least calm it down a little. Or you may just get really drunk, tell more jokes and go home in a cab, waking up with a hangover and a post-mortem anxiety attack (see page 149).

Personalisation

Let's go back to that aforementioned ill-fated dinner party. The personalisation started as soon as you believed that the woman at the end of the table was looking at you and thinking about you. The alternatives were that she was looking at a painting above your head, or that she was simply gazing into space. There was no evidence that she was thinking about you.

Social anxiety does have a weird paradoxical narcissism about it. On the one hand, there is a crippling anxiety which causes you to go out of your way to avoid coming into contact with other people. But in the company of others, you assume that others' attentions are directed at you. Go figure!

The reasonings

This is when you gather information from your senses and your beliefs, and register this information as factual. 'The reasonings' are very powerful thought distortions and they fuel many of the others, as you will discover . . .

Emotional
reasoning

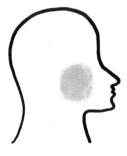

Biological
reasoning

Cognitive
reasoning

Emotional reasoning

This occurs when you convince yourself that because you feel something it must be a fact. David Burns, in his book *Feeling Good* (1980), describes it brilliantly:

Even when your thoughts are distorted they nevertheless create a powerful illusion of truth. Let me expose the basis for this deception in blunt terms—your feelings are not facts! In fact your feelings, per se, don't even count—except as a mirror of the way you are thinking. If your perceptions make no sense, the feeling they create will be as absurd as the images reflected in the trick mirrors at an amusement park. But these abnormal emotions feel just as valid and realistic as the genuine feelings created by undistorted thoughts, so you automatically attribute truth to them.

It's a bit like you with your joke. You decided it was a phenomenal failure and started to feel anxious. As soon as the anxious feeling arrives, this provides you with all the evidence that you need to emphatically believe that people are thinking negatively about

you—judging you—and are going to continue to judge you and tell other people how ridiculous you are. This is all based on a feeling that you have created by negative self-evaluation.

Remember—feelings are *not* facts.

Biological reasoning

This is not dissimilar to the workings of emotional reasoning, but in this scenario what you register are the *physical sensations* of the fight/flight response. For example: increased heart rate, gut disturbance, shallow breathing, and so on. These are often the first things we become aware of in times of distress.

You interpret signals from your biological systems as further evidence that something is terribly wrong.

The something that is wrong, however, is the misperception of your reality as a result of your distorted thinking. Nevertheless, both emotional and biological reasoning further reinforce your belief that other people are judging and rejecting you.

Cognitive reasoning

This is the final component of 'the reasonings'. In this instance you assume that because you are thinking something and you believe what you're thinking, those thoughts must be based in fact. This is not true, the reason being:

Beliefs are *not* facts.

If I were to say to you 'I believe that when I let go of this pencil it will drop to the floor', it is irrelevant whether I believe that or not. It is a **fact** that the pencil will drop, supported by all sorts of scientific evidence such as gravity.

'The reasonings' are very convincing phenomena, but the main point to be remembered when confronted with these experiences is that they are based in **assumption**, not **fact**. Separating beliefs from facts is evidence-based thinking, and is essential to rational thinking.

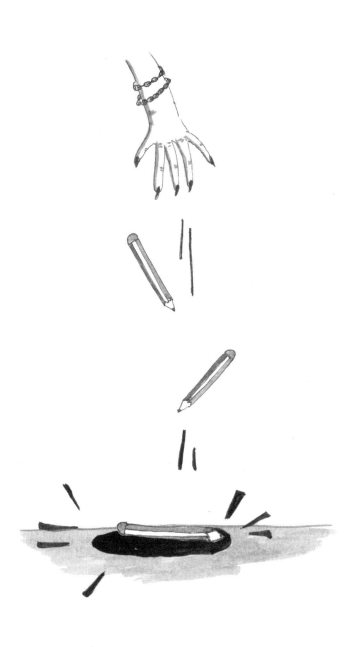

I have one more cluster of thinking errors that I will show you, but not right now. That is enough information for you to be getting on with. Tell you what, we'll run through your homework next time. These early sessions are very educational, but they do provide you with the building blocks and language you will need—I promise.

> **Me**: By the way, don't forget to keep utilising the breathing exercise.
>
> **You**: I bought myself some stickers, and put them around the place like you suggested. It's good—I notice my stomach is starting to settle down a lot.

CHAPTER EIGHTEEN

THERAPY SESSION THREE

Me: Hi again. Nice to see you made it back. How's your brain taking all this new and alien information?

You: Can't say I know quite what to think at the moment. The first session was really straightforward, because I had this name for how I feel and think, whereas last time I just felt a bit confused.

Me: That's cool; you're not doing anything wrong. It is very much like learning a foreign language. You need the words— the jargon—before you can construct a sentence and then a paragraph.

So this is the last group of thinking errors, and then I double-promise we'll get to the practical part of the therapy.

I've kept this cluster until last because they are the most destructive and damaging to your emotional, psychological and physical wellbeing.

They are responsible for, as the French would say, *désaise*—a lack of ease (the origins of our word 'disease').

I like that term because for me it explains psychological ill-health as a function of 'dissing the ease'. Think about how you feel when you are anxious or distressed—your ease of life has been unsettled, as has your emotional state.

So, I would like you to meet the culprits 'Should', 'Must' and 'Have To'.

'SHOULD', 'MUST' AND 'HAVE TO'

I view them like the three witches in Shakespeare's *Macbeth* (AKA the weird sisters)—symbols of dark thought, stirring in their cauldron the emotions of self-loathing, guilt, resentment and anger.

Let me explain in a less theatrical manner. Every time you are thinking, and in particular thinking about yourself, each thought is a silent conversation with the self. Thoughts track through neurological pathways, establishing habits of thought also known as beliefs.

The Should, Must and Have To witches may as

well be considered identical as they all mean the same and create a very similar range of distress. Have a look:

Thoughts	Responses
I should have	guilt / regret
I shouldn't have	guilt / self-loathing
They should have	anger / frustration / disappointment
They shouldn't have	resentment / anger / frustration
I have to	pressure / tension / obligation
I must	more pressure / more tension

This gives a wonderful set of ingredients for the cauldron of 'double, double toil and trouble'. Nothing but dark thoughts, nothing but dark and haunting emotions; all as a result of the Should, Must and Have To witches.

These are control-based words used over the centuries to control populations through guilt in particular—remember 'thou shalt/thou shalt not'. Some people will balk at such a suggestion, as they consider 'should' in particular to be a motivating word. However, the motivation is driven by fear, and this form of motivation will make you ill. True motivation comes from the desire to do or complete something.

It is important to note that not all 'shoulds' are the same. There are two different varieties.

Instructional 'shoulds'

We use these to teach. Children are told that they 'should' never stick objects into a three-point plug socket. This instruction is designed to help minimise the risk of being electrocuted. So it is a helpful 'should'.

Instructional 'shoulds' are also the backbone of instruction manuals, to assemble objects or ensure that your computer is wired up correctly. For instance, you 'must' always switch this on before you activate the software, or the computer will crash. Again, this is helpful and factually based information.

Instructional 'shoulds' are helpful and based in fact.

Moralistic 'shoulds'

Now we enter the danger zone. For example, 'You should do it my way, because my way is the right way'; 'You shouldn't vote for that political party—it is the wrong one'; 'You shouldn't believe in that god because my god is the right one'.

These are value systems, beliefs and expectations, but *they are not based in fact*. Consider it this way:

Question: Whose beliefs are the right ones?
Answer: None of them— beliefs are not facts.

I would very much like you to consider not using the words should/must/have to. Put a radar on your thoughts and be aware of these words, as they begin to impact on your emotions and behaviours, creating pressure and guilt and disappointment— all unpleasant experiences.

They sneak into your brain—sometimes obviously and sometimes not, but they are still there.

This occurs through the process of **inference**.

The 'should statements' can sit in the background—imagine the 'witches' peering out from behind a curtain. You are not conscious of them, but they maintain control of your thoughts via inference, resulting in you taking a meaning from something that is not directly said.

For example, you think to yourself: *That wasn't a very smart thing to say.*

Before you know it, from behind the curtains of your consciousness appear the Should, Must and Have To witches, ready to point the finger and turn the thought into . . .

> 'Did you have to say that? That is the most stupid thing you have ever said. You shouldn't have said that. You must never say anything like that again. People will think you are a complete idiot!'

Ouch! How was that for you? Even typing it left me feeling awful. However, it would have been much worse for you, because you believe those things about yourself. Those Macbeth girls (thinking distortions)

just stir up that cauldron of dark thoughts, leaving you overwhelmed and struggling to breathe.

Evict them. You'll start to feel better immediately.

Me: OK, let's get to that thought record.
You: It's a bit all over the place. I kept getting the columns mixed up.
Me: No problem—this is your first attempt and it's not easy to separate thoughts from feelings. That's because they occur so closely together, making them difficult to differentiate.

You are most likely to register the emotional experiences and biological sensations first, because they are subjectively the most powerful. Just record those responses, then backtrack to the thoughts.

A	B	C

A SITUATION

Took my dog home from the park. He was playing with another dog.

B THOUGHTS

What if that owner gets upset?

She'll tell the other owners about me. They won't let us back at the park.

C FEELINGS

Fearful, stressed, anxious
(SUDS 80%)

C BIOLOGY

Heart pounding, shortness of breath, face went red

C BEHAVIOUR

Picked up dog and ran away. Avoided social media when I got home.

Me: That's a brilliant first attempt.

You: Cool. Seeing it written on the whiteboard though, it looks so silly.

Me: I much prefer that you're honest— that way I get to picture what it was like for you at the time. As I explained to you earlier, the SUDS (Subjective Units of Distress Scale) rating provides me with an indication of how fearful and anxious you were at the time. It's not hard to see why you ran away—that 80 per cent refers to the activation of your fight/flight response. So what came naturally to you in this instance was to follow the adrenaline and run.

You see, it is your anxiety that you are running away from. Nothing else had happened apart from what you had imagined. You were scaring yourself with your own thoughts.

SUMMARY

Firstly, every time you start a thought with 'what if?', you enter into the whirlpool of worrisome overthinking. Off you go, sucked into a vortex of fear and anxiety.

As I mentioned earlier, social anxiety is fuelled by worry, and it all starts with that inoffensive little phrase 'what if?' It is often triggered by uncertainty. In your example, you were clearly unsure of what your dog was going to do and what the owners were going to do in response. Of course, you couldn't tell that, because you are not—I repeat *not*—a mind-reader. However, your assumption was that the outcome was going to be disastrous. Let me show you something:

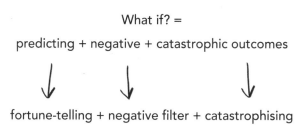

What if? =

predicting + negative + catastrophic outcomes

fortune-telling + negative filter + catastrophising

This simple diagram illustrates the power of the thought distortions, and shows how you made it to 80 per cent on the SUDS. All your predictions were negative and they were huge and frightening and terrible, which is exactly how you ended up feeling.

For a more detailed
understanding of the workings
of 'what if?', grab . . .

Let's do a little more unpacking of that 80 per cent SUDS rating, because it tells me how distressed you felt.

> You are in the park, and you see your dog about to play with another dog. Then, through the cognitive filters of catastrophising and fortune-telling with

a negative filter, you convince yourself that a horrific dog-fight is going to occur. The owner of the other dog is going to judge you and make sure you are banned from the park, and she's going to plaster a warning notice about you all over social media.

Not bad for one quick thought!

The lesson from this is that you have imagined this event and created in your mind a fate almost worse than death. I know it felt real for you, but here you need to remember:

Feelings are not facts.

What is required here is a strategy for perspective. Try this: it is called 'the terribleness scale'.

```
                              (dog in scuffle)
                                    80%
0% ┣━━━━━━━━━━━━━━━━━━━━━━━━━━━━━━━━━┷━━━━━┫ 100%
```

Me: Now I want you to imagine a loved one ending up on life support after being run over by a car. Where would that be on the scale?
You: OMG! Somewhere around 99 per cent!

Me: Mmmm . . . that's worth re-evaluating. The way things are at the moment in your mind, the near-death of a loved one is only 19 units of distress away from your dog getting into an imagined fracas.

Doesn't seem quite right, does it? That's because it isn't. What I have exposed you to here is the usefulness of thinking about a 'real' problem versus some imagined scenario that you have made up.

With this technique, you can draw the scale on a piece of paper, placing the events along the scale, or you can ask yourself the following questions:

How bad is this really?
What is the worst that can happen?

You are asking your brain to define exactly how bad this situation is and, if by chance it does pan out, what is the worst thing that could happen. You will find that asking these questions will bring your distress down considerably.

Asking your brain a question will encourage it to reason and not just react. When given time, the temporal lobe will look for a reason and be distracted from the response of the amygdala (fight/flight).

It's also better to ask your brain a question than to tell it *not to think* something. When you try to tell your brain that it 'shouldn't' think about something, that is the first thing it will do. Remember that camel I stuck in your throat (page 47)? Well, the same thing applies—when you focus on a thought, it will not go away. In fact, quite the opposite—it becomes bigger and harder to ignore.

However, when you take out the 'should not'—as I have suggested—and you ask the brain questions, it will go on a mission to look for the rational. Socrates (who died in 399 BC) was credited with a concept known as 'Socratic dialogue', which forms the backbone of law and cognitive therapy. He referred to the process of 'guided discovery', where, given the right question, the temporal lobe goes looking for the answer based in truth and reason.

TAKEAWAYS FROM TODAY'S SESSION

- Beware the Should, Must and Have To witches! Listen for those words in your thinking.
- Watch out for thoughts that start with 'what if'.
- Remember you are not a mind-reader.
- Use the 'terribleness scale' to help you put things in perspective.

HOMEWORK

That's enough for this session. Just before you go, here is your homework. You'll notice it is a very similar template, but this time you need to fill in column D with any thinking errors you can identify.

| A | B | C | D |

A SITUATION	B THOUGHTS	C FEELINGS	D THINKING ERRORS
		C BIOLOGY	
		C BEHAVIOUR	

Me: Once again, don't be concerned about getting it 'right'—there is no right or wrong, there is only how you feel.

Have a good week, and I'll see you next time with your thought record.

CHAPTER NINETEEN

THERAPY SESSION FOUR

Me: How's things?

You: Good. I found that terribleness scale helpful for calming down and looking more realistically at situations. I also liked that idea 'You're scaring yourself with your own thoughts.'

Me: That's great—how did you use it?

You: I wrote it down on a piece of paper and carried it with me in my wallet, looking at it when I started to feel anxious.

Me: That's fantastic. You have come up with your own way to create what we in the trade call a 'flashcard' . . .

FLASHCARDS

Back in the old days, psychological therapists were primarily trained in the use of behaviour therapies. Then into the mix came the use of visualisations. When trying to assist people with clearing their

minds of unwanted thoughts, we would ask them to visualise a stop sign. This was called 'thought stopping' or 'blocking'.

These were the early stages of the development of flashcards, which are pieces of paper (or files on your phone) which you look at to help develop new, more positive thought patterns. Research tells us that if you are wanting to change the way you think, you need to internalise effectively the new way of thinking. By doing that you have more chance of replacing the old thinking habits. Writing the desired new thought down on a flashcard, to read and remind yourself of it on a regular basis, is a way to rewire the brain.

Here are a few examples (copies of these are included in an appendix at the back of the book—see page 301). You can choose the ones that work best for you.

> # FEELINGS ARE NOT FACTS.
>
> # BELIEFS ARE NOT FACTS.
>
> # I'M SCARING MYSELF WITH MY OWN THOUGHTS.
>
> # PERCEIVED THREATS ARE NOT LIFE-THREATENING.

You can write these out on little pieces of card to carry in your wallet or, as many of my clients do, type them in your phone as a memo.

There is science behind this approach. You are in the process of retraining your brain and creating new neurological pathways. Hence it is essential that you don't just pick up the card, glance at it for a few seconds and then discard it. You need to stare at the card for 10-15 seconds each time for it to have any impact and make change.

You will find these little catchphrases incredibly helpful for stopping that spiral of unwanted thoughts going around and around and around in your head, ad nauseam. Imagine the flashcards as an exit path from this spiral of worrisome overthinking.

As I mentioned earlier, when you ask the brain a question—such as 'How is this thinking helping me?' or 'Where is this thinking taking me?'—it is distracted and goes looking for an answer to the question rather than just attempting to suppress the thoughts (as in 'stop thinking about that camel in your throat').

Me: That's enough on the flashcards. Let's have a look at this week's thought record.

You: I think I've done it right. Sometimes I just get so wound up it is difficult to find the thoughts.

Me: Let's have a look . . .

A	B	C	D

A SITUATION

I said something technically wrong to a junior at work. He responded in a sarcastic manner, 'Mmmm . . . no, I don't think so.'

B THOUGHTS

Now he's going to think I'm an idiot. He's going to bad-mouth me to the boss and tell him I'm not worth the money I'm getting paid. I'm so embarrassed. I should know this stuff! I'm a problem, and I'm not good enough for this job.

C FEELINGS

Overwhelmed, anxious, panicky, fearful, embarrassed (SUDS 80%)

C BIOLOGY

Foggy brain, heart racing, sweating

C BEHAVIOUR

Got defensive, looked away and focused on work, avoided eye contact

D THINKING ERRORS

Mind-reading, fortune-telling, 'should' statements, labelling, emotional reasoning, cognitive reasoning, negative mental filter

Me: Excellent, well done. It's good to see that you already have such a thorough understanding of the thinking errors.

SUMMARY

Once a *meaning* was given to the junior's comment, the stage was set for assumption and distorted interpretations. In this example your thinking errors were primarily to do with believing in feelings.

The feelings of anxiety and embarrassment kicked in, and with that came the **emotional and cognitive reasoning**: 'I feel this way so I must be useless at this job.'

Your fear and panic are also fuelled by **mind-reading** and **fortune-telling**, always with the **negative mental filter** in place, because without that you wouldn't be feeling this way. You started to assume that you knew what he was thinking, and then predicted that he was going to bad-mouth you to your boss. Of course, none of these thoughts were based in fact.

Your negative **labelling** was a direct result of the Macbeth trio (**Should, Must and Have To**): 'I should know this stuff. I must be a problem and I shouldn't have this job,' and so on, and so on.

> **Me**: I hope that all makes sense. The main understanding here is that you are troubling *yourself* by believing in assumptions and feelings. Your goal is to start evaluating your thoughts *based on fact.*

TAKEAWAYS FROM TODAY'S SESSION

- Get into the habit of using flashcards.
- Continue to familiarise yourself with the thinking errors and keep an ear out for 'should' statements.
- Increase your awareness of the falsehood of mind-reading.

HOMEWORK

Complete another thought record using the same template.

CHAPTER
TWENTY

THERAPY
SESSION
FIVE

Me: Hi, nice to see you again. How's everything?

You: Yeah, good. I get what you mean about those flashcards. I've been using them all week and they're really helpful.

I especially like the question 'Is this thinking helping me?' Something will happen and I'll start freaking out and heading into the thought spiral, but as soon as I ask myself that question I realise the answer is 'no', and then I can distract myself. Sometimes I have to do it more than once, but I do get there.

I've also been watching out for those 'Should', 'Must' and 'Have To' sisters. That has been really liberating, as I don't feel so pressured all the time.

I've still been using the breathing exercise, but the most helpful thing is reminding myself that I cannot mind-read.

Me: Sounds like everything is starting to click into place, which is very cool. I know what it's like—there is so much information to take in, and initially it doesn't appear to make any sense at all, but then incrementally the knowledge gets integrated into your mindset and you're away.

Time to have a look at your homework . . .

A	B	C	D

A SITUATION

Being invited to a family wedding, where there will be people who I don't know.

B THOUGHTS

What if I make a bad impression? What if I don't have anything to talk about? I'll ruin something.

C FEELINGS

Anxious (SUDS 75%)

C BIOLOGY

Heart racing, shallow breathing

C BEHAVIOUR

Talked to my parents, asked about the people who will be attending, did the breathing exercises, used my flashcards

D THINKING ERRORS

Negative mental filter, fortune-telling, I can't stand it-itis, magnification, cognitive reasoning

Me: First of all, shit hot! It's so good to see you integrating the techniques to manage your anxiety. How long did you stay at that 75 per cent units of distress?

You: Not long. Talking to my family helped.

SUMMARY

There are three things I would like to comment on here. Firstly, **what if?** is always guaranteed to take you into that anxious spiral. Remember is it based in **fortune-telling** and **catastrophising**, with the ever-present **negative mental filter**. Find an exit from this thought pattern as soon as you can. Flashcards are helpful with that.

Secondly, with regard to your reassurance seeking—it is not a major felony that you spoke to your family members. It may well have been that you were looking for information that would help you navigate the social situation. However, what you do need to avoid doing is *relying on your loved ones to reassure you that you are going to be OK.* If that was your purpose in talking to your parents, then you are still telling yourself that being with other people is dangerous and scary, and that you won't be able to cope.

You have to *learn to reduce your own anxiety.* Relying on other people will only provide you with short-term relief, leaving you dependent on input from others.

THE MYTH OF 'MAKE ME'

I'd like to introduce you to a myth. So often people will say things to me like:

- He made me feel embarrassed.
- She made me feel stupid.
- They made me feel left out.
- He made me angry.

None of these statements is correct. The belief that people *make* you do and feel things is false—it is a myth. It may *feel* as though that is the case, but then of course we know that:

Feelings are not facts.

Let me illustrate this with an example. You and I are sitting in my office on the third floor, next to a window. I tell you that I want you to jump out of the window as a way of leaving the session.

Some 'people-pleasers' will look out of the window, but as yet no one has jumped out, no matter how persuasive I try to be.

You *choose* not to jump out of the window, because you don't want to end up in a back brace with multiple broken limbs. It would be different if I had a gun to your head, because then it would be a choice between instant death and those broken limbs. You evaluate the situation and then *make a choice*. I can't *make* you jump without using aggressive force.

Although it may not feel like it, emotions are the same. I can't *make* you love me, I can't *make* you smile, I can't *make* you cry. *You do that.*

Your thinking dictates what you do and how you feel—nothing and nobody else. People can influence you or have an impact, but it is *your* evaluation of the value of an interaction and the meaning you give it that create your response.

If someone you love doesn't love you back, you need to learn to accept that fact. Stalking and begging are not going to help. Likewise, from the other side, if you don't want to establish or maintain an intimate relationship with someone then they can't make you.

Your thoughts, your choices.
There is no 'make you'.

I want you to really believe this, because by doing so you take back control of your life. There will be no more 'leaf in the wind' behaviour, where you feel like you are constantly being buffeted around by the actions and reactions of others.

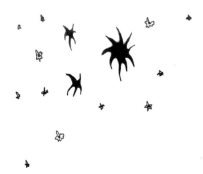

TAKEAWAYS FROM TODAY'S SESSION

- Ease back on the reassurance-seeking.
- Keep using the breathing exercise.
- Keep familiarising yourself with the thinking errors.
- Most importantly, remember that 'make me' is a myth, not a fact of life.

HOMEWORK

I want you to complete another thought record. In our next session we're going to take it to the advanced stage by attempting to challenge your negative thoughts. I'll talk you through how to do that next time—see you then.

CHAPTER
TWENTY-ONE

THERAPY
SESSION SIX

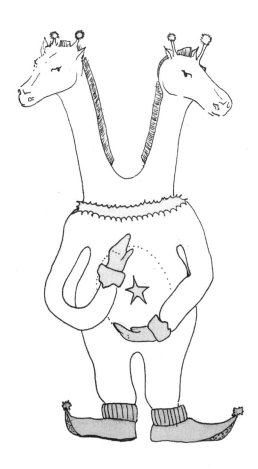

Me: How are you doing?

You: I had a good week. Things are starting to make sense as I practise more of the things you talk to me about.

Me: Anything in particular?

You: Well, I'm still doing the breathing exercise, I like that. I am experimenting with different flashcards in different situations. If I'm getting really anxious before I go out to meet people, I have started using 'I'm scaring myself with my own thoughts'. It helps me decatastrophise. And it helps me remember that my own thoughts are causing my distress, not other peoples' thoughts—because I don't know what they are thinking.

Me: Excellent.

You: One more thing: I quite liked that conversation we had about the myth of 'make me'. Realising that I can choose what

I feel has been giving me more of a sense of control, knowing that understanding the way I think will help me manage my feelings. I always used to believe that my feelings just overwhelmed me and there was nothing I could do about what was happening—that 'leaf in the wind' metaphor.

The main thing I still seem to be having trouble with is that 'what if?' spiral. I try the flashcards—'How is this thinking helping me?' is my favourite, but it doesn't seem to work all the time, especially with the 'what if?' problem.

Me: OK, let me introduce you to another approach . . .

I have found that different flashcards work for different people. And sometimes a card that has worked for a while just seems to lose its 'potency', for no particular reason.

When I am working with my clients, I will often design completely new ones, tailored to the individual. Here is one of my favourites, plus a new one that I have come up with quite recently.

NOT NOW!!!

This is very suitable for the 'what if?' scenario. For example: 'What if she is thinking . . .?' or 'What if he is thinking I'm an idiot and he tells other people?'

The 'Not now!' statement requires the brain to stop worrying, with the promise that it can think those thoughts later in the day. The brain will often be far more accommodating of this message than it will be of 'Stop, you shouldn't think like this'.

The other desirable feature of this flashcard is that it is short and concise. It doesn't take much to remember and it doesn't take long to process. The perfect stopgap!

Along these same lines I came up with another card:

NOT HELPFUL!!!

I especially like this one, because it includes that wonderful word **helpful**. Again, it's shorter than the others. I sometimes find that the more concise cards have that bit of extra grunt.

OK, let's have a look at that thought record of yours . . .

A	B	C	D

A SITUATION

Woke up the morning after my performance review at work.

B THOUGHTS

I can't deal with going into work today. But if I take time off work people will think I'm lazy. They will think I'm unreliable and shouldn't have the job. I can't deal with talking to any of them. They will all be talking about me.

C FEELINGS

Frustration, anxiety (SUDS 60%)

C BIOLOGY

Unsettled stomach, restless sleep

C BEHAVIOUR

Stayed in bed late, did the breathing exercises, used my flashcards

D THINKING ERRORS

Can't stand it-itis, mind-reading, fortune-telling, emotional reasoning, cognitive reasoning, negative mental filter

Me: Cool. The first thing to comment on is that even though you were quite down in the dumps and pissed off, your units of distress (SUDS) sat at 60 per cent. What is good about this is that it seems your baseline distress is not skyrocketing the way that it was.

Great job with the 'spot the thinking errors' game, too. You've got a really good understanding of them now, so let's take it to the next level . . .

RATIONAL ALTERNATIVE THINKING

Thus far we have focused on the distorted negative automatic thoughts that you are consciously aware of. You are becoming more familiar with identifying the thinking errors. This last bit brings all of this knowledge together, teaching you how to formulate **rational alternative thinking**. This rational thinking is the ultimate goal of our therapy.

When you are being guided
by emotion and looking through
distorted lenses, your thinking
is primarily **irrational**: illogical,
absurd, nonsensical, baseless
and unreasonable.

Where you *want* your thinking
to be is in the **rational** camp:
balanced, logical, reasonable,
sound and realistic.

I would like to emphasise that it is *within your interpersonal world* that the brain is most likely to play tricks. Clearly, when interpreting basic information such as 'stop at the red light', 'turn the tap on to get water' and 'chairs are to sit on', the information being transmitted remains within a factual interpretation, with no room for confusion or misinterpretations.

The model shown opposite is the matrix I will use to show you how to maintain rational rather than irrational thinking.

A MATRIX FOR CHALLENGING IRRATIONAL THOUGHTS

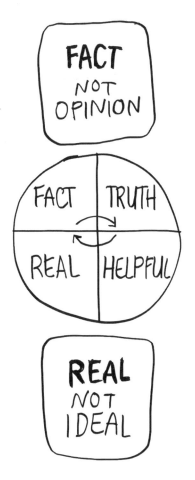

To achieve rational thinking, ask yourself: Is my thinking based in fact, truth and reality? Is my thinking helpful?

Rational thinking is based in fact,
truth and what is real and helpful.

Irrational thoughts are based
in opinion and ideals.

So, let's go through your thought record and see what we come up with.

I can't deal with going into work today.

So, you are telling yourself that. Is it *true* that the performance review is the worst experience you have ever had in your life? Probably not, so the fact is you are able to go into work today.

But if I take time off work people will think I am lazy.

Is it a fact that you can read people's minds? Absolutely not! And if in the real world you found out that people in the office were thinking that you were lazy, is this a fact or their opinion?

They will think I'm unreliable and shouldn't have the job.

Here again you are relying on your fictional belief that you can mind-read—not true. With this thought you have also entered into fortune-telling—predicting what people will be thinking in the future. This is not a fact either.

With regards to the 'should statement', again, if this person was in fact thinking that (which you don't *know*), that would be their opinion and also based in their ideals about how people should behave in the workplace.

I can't deal with talking to any of them.

Again, another 'I can't stand it'. Also not true, because you talk to these people every other day that you are there. You have frightened yourself by thinking that they're thinking negatively about you and they want to see you get fired—mind-reading with a negative mental filter and emotional reasoning.

They will all be talking about me.

You do not know what they are thinking and you certainly do not know what they might be thinking about you. Your use of the word *all* suggests that *everybody* will be doing this, creating in your mind an even spookier scenario. So now it is everybody (all-or-nothing thinking) who is thinking negatively about you, and you believe this to be true (cognitive reasoning)—that's belief, not fact.

> **Me**: Can you see what is going on here with these thoughts? Out of a total of five thoughts none of them are based in fact, hence you are believing in thoughts that are not true.
>
> **You**: I can see that now. It's a bit embarrassing actually, seeing it written down. But how do I think differently? I do know my thoughts are irrational, but I still keep thinking like that.
>
> **Me**: Well, that's going to be this week's homework . . .

TAKEAWAYS FROM TODAY'S SESSION

- Practise using NOT NOW!!! and NOT HELPFUL!!! for spiralling negative thoughts, particularly those thoughts that start with 'what if?'
- Focus on thinking **rationally**, not **irrationally**. Use the matrix for rational thinking and ask yourself: Is my thinking based in fact, truth and reality? Is my thinking helpful?
- Don't think and behave like a leaf in the wind.

HOMEWORK

For your homework this week I'd like you to fill in a new thought record, but this time you're going to have a go at replacing your irrational thoughts with more rational ones. You can add a column E for this, if you like, or you can just jot the alternative thoughts down in a new list.

> **Me**: Just see how you get on—it's not a performance review. I'll talk you through anything you get stuck with. See you next time, with your thought record. Have a great week.

CHAPTER TWENTY-TWO

THERAPY SESSION SEVEN

Me: Hi there. Well, you may or may not be pleased to know that this is our last session together.

(Just to return to the real world for a minute and not our little imaginary one, you should know that *it is not failing* if you make contact for the odd follow-up session after a course of therapy—it's no different to getting a warrant of fitness for your car or going to the dentist for a check-up. Realistically, your anxiety will never be completely 'fixed', and you may need ongoing help managing it. The beauty of *The Book of Angst* is that it is only ever a reach of the arm away. You can dip in and out of the book if you get stuck or forget something we have covered. One of my clients said to me recently, referring to *The Book of Overthinking*, 'I always know where it is, and I often take it out with me—it has become like a little friend.' This was a wonderful compliment, and I hope *The Book of Angst* becomes the same for you.)

Me: Back to business. How's your week been?

You: I'm really starting to get it now. I still have my favourite flashcards, but I have been using NOT NOW!!! and that really helps. I'm still doing the breathing, and using the matrix if I am trying to assess whether or not my thinking is rational.

Me: That's cool, well done. Here's another catchphrase that you may find a bit speedier than referring back to the matrix, especially if you are out somewhere:

IS THIS THINKING TRUE?
IS IT BASED IN FACT?

Me: That covers a lot of ground in the one flashcard! Give it a try. Now, let's have a look at your thought record . . .

A

A SITUATION

My newish girlfriend, Chrissy, wants me to meet her parents.

B

B THOUGHTS

They will think I'm not good enough for their daughter. They won't like me.
I will say something stupid.
I won't know what to talk about.
I will embarrass myself and then I will embarrass Chrissy.
Then she will want to finish the relationship.
I won't be able to handle it.
It will end in disaster.

C

C FEELINGS

Anxious, fearful, inferior (SUDS 80%)

C BIOLOGY

Racing heart, sweaty palms, upset stomach

C BEHAVIOUR

Didn't answer immediately, tried to avoid the conversation, started to worry

D

D THINKING ERRORS

Mind-reading, negative mental filter, I can't stand it-itis, catastrophising, fortune-telling, all the 'reasonings'

Me: OK. And how did you get on with the alternative thoughts?

You: I found those quite difficult, but here goes . . .

- I can't predict what they will think of me.
- I can't mind-read, so I have no idea what they are thinking.

Me: Excellent. Now I'm going to explain to you a few more ways to understand and work with these techniques. Firstly, let's take a look at your negative automatic thoughts:

- They will think I'm not good enough for their daughter.
- They won't like me.
- I will say something stupid.
- I won't know what to talk about.
- I will embarrass myself and then I will embarrass Chrissy.
- Then she will want to finish the relationship.
- I won't be able to handle it.
- It will end in disaster.

Me: They're full of thought distortions, hence neither true nor factual. They're not based in reality nor helpful, hence totally irrational. Now let's examine the make-up of your alternative thoughts:

- I can't predict what they will think of me = TRUE
- I can't mind-read, so I have no idea what they are thinking = FACT

IRRATIONAL	RATIONAL
(SUDS 80%)	I can't predict what they will think of me = **TRUE**
They will think I'm not good enough for their daughter.	I can't mind-read, so I have no idea what they are thinking = **FACT**
They won't like me.	
I will say something stupid.	
I won't know what to talk about.	
I will embarrass myself and then I will embarrass Chrissy.	
Then she will want to finish the relationship.	
I won't be able to handle it.	
It will end in disaster.	

Me: That's more like it! Now let's compare and re-evaluate your distress ratings. First, let's focus on the rational thoughts column and rate your units of distress. This is how we start to really see your progress.

You: After coming up with those alternative thoughts, my SUDS rating has gone down. But I still struggle to believe that I will be OK.

Me: Just pause for a moment and remember a few of your flashcards. For instance . . .

WHAT'S THE WORST
THAT CAN HAPPEN?

I'M SCARING MYSELF
WITH MY OWN THOUGHTS.

Me: Now focus again on the rational thinking—thinking that is based in fact. Try again.

You: Mmmm . . . probably 35 to 40 per cent. It's much less, I know, but I'm still not totally relaxed.

Me: I guess the thing with a situation like this is that it would be somewhat uncomfortable for *most* people, not just you because you have a fear of being judged. Due to all the things we have talked about—including epigenetics—your *subjective experience of anxiety* will be more intense. However, remember that a certain apprehension about such a meeting is to be expected.

ANOTHER EXERCISE YOU MIGHT LIKE TO TRY

Before going into a situation where you have significant 'anticipatory anxiety' (anxiety in anticipation), complete a thought record.

This can help you rationalise your thoughts,

reducing your anxiety before the event.

Then, after you have been through the 'ordeal', do another one and take note of the difference. No doubt what you imagined will be far from what actually happened in the real world. The benefit of doing this can also stretch to helping you minimise the **post-mortem anxiety** if there was a bit of a *faux pas* (remember that one—it's French for f@ck-up).

This little technique is a way of providing you with ongoing feedback and evidence of your progress, as well as reminding you of the destructive power of irrational thought.

> **You**: Another good idea—I'll give that one a whirl.
>
> **Me**: Let's have a look at today's takeaway before we say goodbye. In the back of this book I'm going to provide a full summing-up for you, so you can easily access the information that you have found the most helpful.

TAKEAWAYS FROM TODAY'S SESSION

- If you have been having therapy, it's also OK to go back for another appointment. Dealing with anxiety requires learning how to manage and enhance your life. Just like asthma and diabetes, there is no 'cure' as such.
- Remind yourself that irrational thinking is untrue and unhelpful. Focus on rational thinking.
- When you compile your list of rational thoughts, re-rate your units of distress and compare these with how you felt when you were thinking the irrational thoughts.
- If you are faced with a difficult situation, do a 'pre' and 'post' thought record.

None of my books act as an alternative to therapy, and this one is no exception. But for those of you unable to access or afford therapy it's a good start.

As always, I do recommend that if the book has made no difference, you strongly consider seeking professional help.

Me: Well, that's us for now. It has been a pleasure helping you. Take care of yourself and start having some fun.

IMPORTANT STUFF TO REMEMBER

LIGHTBULB

MOMENTS!

ere is a summary of the key points from our sessions, including those 'lightbulb moments' that have hopefully occurred—flashes of clarity, sudden realisations and new ideas that have inspired you and contributed to your progress.

1. The head is attached to the shoulders, so all the components that make us humans who we are—biology, emotions, thoughts and behaviour—are inextricably linked.

2. Medications can be helpful for handling some aspects of your condition, but CBT is the best treatment for anxiety.

3. There is a genetic influence on/contribution to your anxiety. You have not brought it on yourself.

4. Your anxiety can be triggered both internally and externally. Your own thinking can and does switch

on your fight/flight mechanism.

5. 'What if?' thinking is a very potent trigger for all forms of anxiety, including social anxiety.

6. Irrational thoughts create exaggerated emotions because you believe them to be true.

A = Reality (this is not the problem)
B = Thinking (this is where
the therapy occurs)
C = Responses: emotions/
biology/behaviour (this is
where the problems lie)
B (thinking) creates C (responses)

---

7. The brain can and does lie to you. Thinking errors allow this to happen. You must memorise them so you can recognise them! (Refer to pages 209-238.)

8. If you know how you think, you can change how you feel.

9. It's OK to be an introvert—some people are born with that temperament. The goal of therapy is *not* to become an extrovert. The goal is to be comfortable in your own skin.

10. 'Make me' is a myth. *You* make you think, feel and behave.

11. Reassurance-seeking leaves you dependent on others to feel OK, so is only a temporary fix.

12. Safety behaviours do not work—they maintain your fear.

13. Decatastrophising is a quick and easy method for calming yourself down. Don't forget to use the 'terribleness scale'.

14. Breathing exercises (see page 200) can help calm your nervous system and distract you from your self-critical mind-chatter.

15. Rational thinking is based in fact, truth and what is real and helpful.

16. Irrational thoughts are based in opinions and ideals. Use the matrix (see page 277) to help you differentiate irrational and rational thoughts.

17. *Helpful* is a neutral and gentle word. Apply it as often as you can when assessing the content and meaning of your thoughts.

18. Share what you are learning with your loved ones, so they can better understand what you experience. They are closest to you, and this knowledge will undoubtedly explain a lot of your previous avoidant behaviour.

19. No matter how much you love someone and feel close to them, you cannot read their mind, and they cannot read yours. You are not, and will never be, a mind-reader!

FLASHCARDS

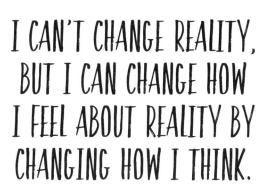

I CAN'T CHANGE REALITY,
BUT I CAN CHANGE HOW
I FEEL ABOUT REALITY BY
CHANGING HOW I THINK.

SOMETHING FALSE CAN FEEL VERY
TRUE. I MUSTN'T LET A FEELING
CONVINCE ME IT'S A FACT.

PERCEIVED THREATS ARE
NOT LIFE-THREATENING.

WHERE IS THIS THINKING
TAKING ME?

- - - - - - - - - - - - -

HOW IS THIS THINKING
HELPING ME?

- - - - - - - - - - - - -

IS MY THINKING TRUE?

- - - - - - - - - - - - -

FEELINGS ARE NOT FACTS.
BELIEFS ARE NOT FACTS.

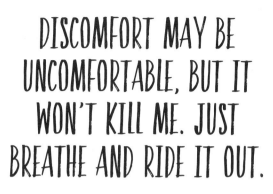

DISCOMFORT MAY BE UNCOMFORTABLE, BUT IT WON'T KILL ME. JUST BREATHE AND RIDE IT OUT.

- -

NOT NOW!!!

- -

NOT HELPFUL!!!

- -

I'M SCARING MYSELF WITH MY OWN THOUGHTS.

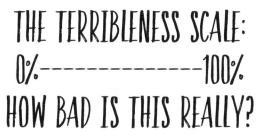

THE TERRIBLENESS SCALE:
0%---------------100%
HOW BAD IS THIS REALLY?

- - - - - - - - - - -

FACT VS. OPINION

- - - - - - - - - - -

DONE IS BETTER THAN PERFECT.

- - - - - - - - - - -

CHOOSE THE THOUGHTS
THAT ARE HELPFUL.

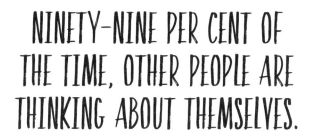

NINETY-NINE PER CENT OF
THE TIME, OTHER PEOPLE ARE
THINKING ABOUT THEMSELVES.

- - - - - - - - - - - - - - - - -

I MAKE ME FEEL.
OTHER PEOPLE AND REALITY
ARE NOT RESPONSIBLE
FOR HOW I FEEL.

- - - - - - - - - - - - - - - - -

I AM NOT, AND WILL NEVER
BE, A MIND-READER.